NOVELS BY MONROE ENGEL

A Length of Rope

The Visions of Nicholas Solon

The Maturity of Dickens

The MATURITY of
DICKENS

Monroe Engel

Cambridge, Massachusetts
HARVARD UNIVERSITY PRESS
OXFORD UNIVERSITY PRESS, LONDON
1959

© 1959 by Monroe Engel

Printed in the United States of America

To the memory of Francis Otto Matthiessen
and
for my daughter Robin

PREFACE

Much of the professed esteem for Dickens is uneasy esteem, exacted rather than willingly given or believed in. Not all, of course. Edmund Wilson, most notably among recent critics, has made and supported claims for Dickens comparable to the claims made for him earlier by Gissing and Chesterton. No one writing about Dickens now, least of all myself, can be sure of the extent of his debt to Wilson's seminal essay in *The Wound and the Bow*, except to know that it is considerable. The usual pattern of Dickens criticism, however, has involved a fluent recital of his faults and limitations smothering a very limited declaration of his greatness. Critics who take this line really grant him importance only piously, because of their recognition that somehow, even if unreasonably, he continues to exercise an imaginative hold on any readers who genuinely attempt him. Not untypical in this regard is Mario Praz, who, in *The Hero in Eclipse in Victorian Fiction*, follows a conventional enough elaboration of Dickens' failures, including his failure to deal realistically with sex, with the assertion that he has interest for us nevertheless as a writer of sketches or fictional essays.

This kind of patronizing scrappy praise must seem insufficient to anyone convinced that Dickens is one of the greatest of English novelists. The size and variety of his achievement, as well as its power for vital survival, point to the need for some more substantial terms of recognition. It is time to concede Dickens' faults — though with reservations — and spend space and effort instead on an assessment of the intention and technique that shape his novels. For these purposes it will hardly do to examine one or two of the novels alone, for the crucial aspect of Dickens' achievement is the absolute continuity of his commitments and materials, but the astonishing range and development within that continuity.

By considering all the novels, and considering them more or less chronologically, it is possible to see the increasing consciousness and control of Dickens' artistry, as for example in the multiple construction he comes characteristically to employ: the immediate control of the intricate plots and of the great social themes with their bearing symbols, and the less overt control of the obsessional private themes, which have in turn their own bearing symbols. Thus in *Our Mutual Friend*, the last completed novel, the social or public themes are informed by the money-dust analogy, and the private themes by the symbolic use of the river. But these public and private themes are not exclusive. They relate to and support each other, and it is on precisely this connection that much of Dickens' genius and power as a novelist depend.

A recurrent purpose of the pages that follow is to show the nature of the multiple construction in the novels starting with *Dombey and Son* (1846–48). The fiction of the first third of Dickens' career will be treated rather summarily. This is not intended to denigrate the early work. Though taste now seems to favor the later, more coherent novels, George H. Ford's *Dickens and His Readers*: *Aspects of Novel-Criticism Since 1836* makes it clear that most of Dickens' contemporaries were of a different mind, and thought these later novels a falling off from the exuberant spontaneity of the earlier books. But I am interested to show the increasing extent to which Dickens became a conscious artist, and this interest is served more clearly by the later novels than by his fiction of the thirties and early forties. Conversely, of course, I may be eschewing what would be a harder job: a particular assessment of the qualities of a natural genius. It would be a greater challenge to current literary fashion too, to prescribe for the earlier fiction the kind of reading it deserves.

I mean my title, "The Maturity of Dickens," to do double work — not only to indicate that the later novels are my primary concern, but to insist that Dickens can and should be read with pleasure and no restriction of intelligence by post-Jamesian adults. In justice to him and to ourselves, he should be read in childhood, and then again when we are grown and can see that the fabulous world discovered to us when we were young is in fact the real world in which we live and suffer.

For Dickens is a realistic novelist in all but superficialities, and even superficially is more often realistic than the twentieth century reader can appreciate, as Humphry House, for example, has shown in *The Dickens World*. He was also, and relatedly, a highly intentional novelist, and any reading of his novels without some understanding of his intentions is an unnecessarily partial reading. I attempt to indicate something of these intentions initially in two ways: by an investigation first of his artistic beliefs and then of his social beliefs. Thereafter, I offer a largely thematic consideration of the fiction previous to *Dombey and Son,* and then go on to consider the mature novels in three groups:

A. The Sense of Society: *Dombey and Son, Bleak House, Little Dorrit, Our Mutual Friend.*

B. The Sense of Self: *David Copperfield, Great Expectations.*

C. The Sports of Plenty: *Hard Times, A Tale of Two Cities, The Mystery of Edwin Drood.*

I wish to acknowledge my indebtedness to Professors E. D. H. Johnson, Louis Landa, Carlos Baker, and Jacob Viner of Princeton University, who read or advised me on portions of this book at an early stage; to Mrs. Madeline House who very kindly gave me information about unpublished Dickens letters; to the Pierpont Morgan Library, the Huntington Library, the Berg Collection of the New York Public Library, and the Houghton Library, for the opportunity to examine unpublished Dickens materials.

An earlier version of Chapter I appeared in *Modern Philology;* of Chapter II, in *PMLA.* Portions of Chapter IV are incorporated in the Introduction to the Norton Library edition of *Our Mutual Friend.*

M. E.

Cambridge, Massachusetts
September 1958

CONTENTS

PART ONE ~

He saw everything he related. It passed before him, as he spoke, so vividly, that, in the intensity of his earnestness, he presented what he described to me, with greater distinctness than I can express. I can hardly believe, writing now long afterwards, but that I was actually present in these scenes; they are impressed upon me with such an astonishing air of fidelity.

David Copperfield, Chapter 51

Chapter One

THE STRATEGY OF THE NOVEL

Some artists are both programmatic and highly self-conscious, and, not content with producing art, they also give us the theory or rationale that lies behind and dignifies that art. Others, no less original necessarily, seem to find pleasure in denying that they have either special purpose or special method. Dickens falls somewhere between these two extremes. He never produces in one place a literary theory or key to his method as a novelist, and he rarely talks at length about his writing. Here and there in his letters to his friends, however, or in correspondence in regard to contributions for his magazines *Household Words* and *All the Year Round*, or in occasional statements in those magazines, remarks are made about art that, when taken together, constitute principles remarkable for their coherence and illuminating his own practice.[1] In his early novels, Dickens certainly

---

[1] The two chief published collections of letters are *The Letters of Charles Dickens*, ed. Walter Dexter (Bloomsbury: Nonesuch, 1938), 3 vols., and *The Heart of Charles Dickens: As Revealed in His Letters to Angela Burdett-Coutts*, ed. Edgar Johnson (New York, 1952). Hereafter, these editions will be designated as *Letters* and *Coutts Letters*. Many unpublished letters are quoted or alluded to in Edgar Johnson,

wrote much from "feel," depending on a rich inventive power to supply him as he went along. The later novels are far more planned, however, and it is possible to get an understanding of the outlines of a theory that lies behind them (and only to a lesser extent behind the earlier, more spontaneous novels) by an examination of these remarks and statements on art.

Nothing confuses our view of Dickens more than his great popularity, which was not merely granted but obstinately sought. What confuses us is the present, seemingly ever increasing distance between popular and serious writing, and between their respective audiences, and our suspicion therefore that any writing that is popular must also be inferior, vulgar. Serious writers tend no longer even to confess their desire for an audience. Yet the serious-popular schism is not essential, has not always pertained, and does not entirely pertain even now.

Dickens was peculiarly fitted, by disposition and attitude as well as by ambition, to be a popular writer. For one thing, in part because success came to him so quickly, he had no feelings of natural antagonism toward his audience. Very nearly the only requirement he made of his readers was that they follow their own likings and form their own judgments, and not merely accept the judgments of others.[2] He had a tenderness of concern for his readers perhaps related to that tenderness he believed

---

Charles Dickens: His Tragedy and Triumph (New York, 1952), 2 vols., designated as Johnson.

For Dickens' magazines, the following designations will be used: *HW* for *Household Words, HN* for *The Household Narrative,* and *AYR* for *All the Year Round.*

[2] "To Think, or Be Thought For?" *HW*, XIV (13 September 1856), 193–98, makes this point in regard to painting.

a writer should feel for the characters of whom he writes. This high value of tenderness in literature is something to which he repeatedly returns. He preferred *Humphry Clinker* to "*Peregrine Pickle* and *Roderick Random,* both extraordinarily good in their way, which is a way without tenderness."[3] His judgment of *Robinson Crusoe* was similarly founded. He was puzzled by its popularity, since it "could make no one laugh and could make no one cry." He said that "there [was] not in literature a more surprising instance of an utter want of tenderness and sentiment, than the death of Friday"; and that the "second part . . . [was] perfectly contemptible, in the glaring defect that it exhibits the man who was 30 years on that desert island with no visible effect made on his character by that experience." Significantly, he cites "poor dear Goldsmith" as having the same opinion of *Crusoe.*[4] To the writers whom he knew, and who de-

[3] *Letters* II, 560, to Stone, 30 May 1854. It is remarkable how few books are referred to in Dickens' correspondence, aside from books by writers with whom he was associated in some way or those famous books he read when he was a boy, and which Copperfield reads: *Roderick Random, Peregrine Pickle, Humphry Clinker, Tom Jones, The Vicar of Wakefield, Don Quixote, Gil Blas, Robinson Crusoe, The Arabian Nights,* and *The Tales of the Genii.* Also, unlike Copperfield, he seems to have read the *Tatler,* the *Spectator,* the *Idler,* the *Citizen of the World,* and Mrs. Inchbald's *Collection of Farces* (see Johnson, pp. 20–22; also T. W. Hill, "Books That Dickens Read," *Dickensian,* XLV [1949], 81–90, 201–07). When he did mention other books, it was more likely than not in letters to Forster, whose combination of learning, pomposity, and aggressiveness often seemed a threat to him. Thus in a couple of years in the early forties, he told Forster that Browning's *Blot on the Scutcheon* "has thrown me into a perfect passion of sorrow" (*Letters* I, 490); that "the Shakespeare you bought for me in Liverpool" is "an unspeakable source of delight . . . to me" (*ibid.,* 415); that he had been reading Tennyson (*ibid.,* 473); that he had been reading DeFoe (*sic*) and, again, Tennyson, whom he called "a great creature" (*ibid.,* 623).

[4] *Letters* II, 767–68, to Forster, 1856.

pended heavily on his opinion, he gave praise where he
found tenderness, blame where he did not. He told one
writer that he had ruined a story by being too smart and
patronizing and not having sufficient feeling for the simple people he described; [5] and he told Wilkie Collins that
The Woman in White was an advance over his previous
writing "most especially in respect of tenderness." [6]

Dickens' compassion for the lot of the average poor
Englishman — a compassion that was as constant as
breath for him — fostered the conviction that he had a
responsibility to amuse his readers, whatever else. He
saw no reason for "the English . . . the hardest-worked
people on whom the sun shines," to give their attention
"in their wretched intervals of pleasure" to any art that
did not amuse them.[7] In other, more critical ways too,
he heeded public taste. In 1846, he told a political writer
that "nothing is got by defying the Public." [8] To believe this is, of course, to limit or curb art. Sometimes
the curbs can be rationalized as what art too requires.
Suggesting changes in the interest of popular taste to his
contributors, Dickens tried as often as he could to make
the two demands come together. In asking for some
change to the ending of a story, he wrote:

I particularly entreat you to consider the catastrophe. You
write to be read, of course. The close of the story is unnecessarily painful — will throw off numbers of persons who would
otherwise read it, and who (as it stands) will be deterred by
hearsay from so doing, and is so tremendous a piece of severity, that it will defeat your purpose.[9]

[5] *Letters* II, 851–52, to Stone, 1 June 1857.
[6] *Letters* III, 145, 7 January 1860.
[7] *Letters* II, 548, to Knight, 17 March 1854.
[8] *Letters* I, 742, to Saville, 18 March 1846.
[9] *Letters* II, 679, to Jolly, 17 July 1855.

His disposition to have his own stories end happily is similar. It was a disposition, not a rule, so that he could write an unhappy ending for *Great Expectations*, but abandon it when Bulwer-Lytton objected that it would keep people from reading the book. What he could not abide was a gratuitously unhappy ending. Of a story by Mrs. Gaskell, "The Hearty John Middleton," he wrote that "if it had ended happily (which is the whole meaning of it) [it] would have been a great success. As it is, it ... will not do much, and will link itself painfully, with the girl who fell down at the well, and the child who tumbled downstairs. I wish to Heaven her people would keep a little firmer on their legs!" [10] Nothing in the craft of fiction is so much affected by convention as the creation of a fitting and acceptable ending for a story. There is a tendency to consider the conventional unhappy ending serious, the conventional happy ending frivolous. The distinction is questionable, however; and it is certain that the creation of a credible happiness is more difficult.

Dickens was himself in many ways a representative Englishman. He shared the common English aversion to extremes, in art as in politics, as can be seen for example in the instructions he gave his sub-editor, W. H. Wills, for editing an article by Wilkie Collins:

... look well to Wilkie's article about the Wigan schoolmaster, and not to leave anything in it that may be sweeping, and unnecessarily offensive to the middle class. He has always a tendency to overdo that — and such a subject gives him a fresh temptation. Don't be afraid of the Truth, in the least; but don't be unjust.[11]

[10] *Letters* II, 250, to Wills, 12 December 1850.
[11] *Letters* III, 58, 24 September 1858.

He knows what will offend the middle-class Englishman here, because he is himself offended. There are other ways, however, in which the middle-class strictures, though he heeded them and had even a natural impulse in their favor,[12] also plagued him. He had, for example, to write a preface to *Oliver Twist*, defending his depiction of the sordid lives of the underworld characters by saying that any other, less accurate, depiction would be an encouragement to a life of crime, and pointing out that he had been careful not to let the language of these characters be offensive. The difficulty of the conflict is perhaps clearest when he attacks John Forster's contention that the characters in English novels are uninteresting by contrast with those in French novels:

I have always a fine feeling of the honest state into which we have got, when some smooth gentleman says to me or to some one else when I am by, how odd it is that the hero of an English book is always uninteresting — too good — not natural, &c. I am continually hearing this of Scott from English people here [Paris], who pass their lives with Balzac and Sand. But O my smooth friend, what a shining impostor you must think yourself and what an ass you must think me, when you suppose that by putting a brazen face upon it you can blot out of my knowledge the fact that this same unnatural young gentleman (if to be decent is to be necessarily unnatural), whom you meet in those other books and in mine, *must be*

12 This natural impulse is evidenced in many ways. See, for example, the two-part article on Balzac in *All the Year Round*, which, though it praises his genius, accepts and condones the fact that his later novels were little known in England because their subject matter was repellent ("Portrait of an Author, Painted by His Publisher," *AYR*, I [18 June 1859], 184–89, [25 June 1859], 205–10). In a letter to Wilkie Collins in reference to Charles Reade's controversial novel *Griffith Gaunt*, Dickens also sets hard limits on how much seamy material may be admitted into fiction (*Letters* III, 510–11, 20 February 1867).

presented to you in that unnatural aspect by reason of your morality, and is not to have, I will not say any of the indecencies you like, but not even any of the experiences, trials, perplexities, and confusions inseparable from the making or unmaking of all men.[13]

The protest against unnatural limitations is bitter, but it also contains its own curious counter-protest, in the parenthetical remark about decency and unnaturalness.

The statement of intentions in the first number of *Household Words*,[14] "A Preliminary Word," indicates the nature of Dickens' will to engage with reality in a palatable way:

No mere utilitarian spirit, no iron binding of the mind to grim realities, will give a harsh tone to our Household Words . . . we would tenderly cherish that light of Fancy which is inherent in the human breast. . . . To show to all, that in all familiar things, even in those which are repellant on the surface, there is Romance enough, if we will find it out.

He felt keenly that the artist had a responsibility to discover and show beauty in ordinary life. This same first volume of *Household Words* has an attack on the Pre-Raphaelite Brotherhood for the antielevated calculated ugliness of its pictures: the P.R.B. is accused of turning against nature and what is natural and is likened in absurdity to a medical society founded to protest against the circulation of blood.[15]

[13] *Letters* II, 797, 15 August 1856.
[14] *HW*, I (30 March 1850), ascribed to Dickens in F. G. Kitton, *The Minor Writings of Charles Dickens: A Bibliography and Sketch* (London, 1900).
[15] "Old Lamps for New Ones," *HW*, I (15 June 1850), 265–67, ascribed to Dickens in Kitton.

The "Preliminary Word" shows a kind of Words-
worthian romanticism in its promise to show "familiar
things" in the "light of Fancy." In his preface to *Bleak
House* also, Dickens said, "I have purposely dwelt upon
the romantic side of familiar things." The aims and
achievements of the Romantics were, of course, still a
force in literature,[16] and Dickens will assert that there
is potential interest in everything we see, if we have the
power properly to see it;[17] and that the modern poet or
man of imagination must even find a special beauty in
the ugliness of the world — in, for example, the railway.[18]

What is being asked finally, of course, is a meeting of
art with life which takes account of more than a select
and suitable part of life. There is a striking conjunction
in the *Household Narrative* of lurid accounts of crime,
accident, and disaster with book notes of a high order
of seriousness. When the *Edinburgh Review* attacked
novelists and novels — including *Little Dorrit* — for
their unfitting concern with the problems of contemporary life, Dickens came aggressively to the defense of
just such fiction.[19] Dickens had, in fact, little patience

[16] It will not do to posit any real separation between the Romantics
and the Victorians. For example, one of Dickens' sons is named for
Dickens' good friend Walter Savage Landor; Francis Jeffrey was one of
the first critics to support Dickens; and Samuel Rogers' breakfasts were
his first experience of literary society. The personal links reach back.
Rogers had seen Garrick act, met Johnson and Boswell, Fox, Burke,
Sheridan, and Mme. de Staël, and was a friend of Tom Moore (see
Johnson, p. 229).

[17] "Twenty Miles," *HW*, X (2 September 1854), 68–72.

[18] "Poetry on the Railway," *HW*, XI (2 June 1855), 414–18.

[19] "Curious Misprint in the *Edinburgh Review*," *HW*, XVI (1 August
1857), 97–100, ascribed to Dickens in Kitton. The article in the *Edinburgh Review* was entitled "The License of Modern Novelists."

with any art that did not make terms with what he considered to be reality. *Household Words* attacked the failure of polite and conventional painting to deal with the
rude diversity of life.[20] *All the Year Round*, a decade
later, asserted a reciprocal relationship between the matter of art and the matter of life: fact anticipates fiction and vice versa.[21]

Dickens is likely to start a work of fiction easily but
end it with difficulty. Partly this is caused by progressive
involvement. Even in his late years that same beginning
with spontaneous ease — i.e., inspiration — was sometimes available to him, as when the character of Dr. Marigold "came flashing up in the most cheerful manner and
I had only to look on and leisurely describe it." [22] Of
course, it may be this very quality of inspiration that
helps to create his involvement; but, no matter what the
reason, no other writer of fiction has lived more in the
world he has himself created. His difficulties in killing
off Little Nell and Paul Dombey are by now part of the
Dickens legend.[23] Less known and more impressive are
his remarks in a letter to Forster written as he was finishing *David Copperfield:* "I am within three pages of the
shore; and am strangely divided, as usual in such cases,
between sorrow and joy. Oh, my dear Forster, if I were
to say half of what *Copperfield* makes me feel to-night,
how strangely, even to you, I should be turned inside out!
I seem to be sending some part of myself into the

[20] "An Idea of Mine," *HW*, XVII (13 March 1858), 289–91.
[21] "The Poetry of Fact," *AYR*, XVIII (14 September 1867), 277–
79.
[22] *Letters* III, 438, to Forster, September 1865.
[23] The difficulties over Little Nell were shared by a large public (see
Johnson, pp. 303–04).

Shadowy World." [24] It is not just the autobiographic character of *David Copperfield* that makes for this involvement, as Dickens is at some pains in the letter to make clear.

Despite the radical differences in Dickens' novels,[25] the worlds of those novels have much in common with each other, even as they have much common reference to Dickens' own life and world. Some things about his method of work must have contributed to this relationship. He had, for example, the curious habit of reading his own work for inspiration when he was about to start something new; [26] or he reread *David Copperfield* while working on *Great Expectations*, to be sure he "had fallen into no unconscious repetitions . . . and was affected by it to a degree you would hardly believe." [27] The boundaries between his life and his fiction are fluid in many ways. Very close to the names of characters in his novels are the nicknames he is constantly inventing for his children — Lucifer Box, Mild Glo'ster, Flaster Floby, Young Skull; [28] or the wild profusion of related nicknames for young Edward Bulwer-Lytton Dickens — Plorn, Plornish, Plornish-ghenter, Plornish-maroon, Plornish-Maroon-ti-Goonter.[29] *Household Words*, as part

[24] *Letters* II, 240, 21 October 1850.

[25] The tendency has been to find Dickens writing one or two types of novel over and over again. Edmund Wilson reflects a more careful reading, however, when he says (p. 74): "Dickens never really repeats himself: his thought makes a consistent progress, and his art, through the whole thirty-five years of his career, keeps going on to new materials and effects." "Dickens: The Two Scrooges," in *The Wound and the Bow* (New York, 1941), pp. 1–104.

[26] *Letters* I, 247, to Forster, 12 February 1840.

[27] *Letters* III, 186, to Forster, October 1860.

[28] *Letters* I, 480, to Austin, 25 September 1842.

[29] Johnson, Index, p. clxxvii.

of the continued attack on snobbery, ridicules the changing of names because of snobbery or for euphony and
defends the homely and peculiar English names of the
sort Dickens is most likely to give to his characters.[30]
In his letters he sometimes invents for characters from
his novels speeches that are pertinent to the subject he
is discussing, as though these characters were real people
with opinions to be consulted.

It must be understood — for it has great relevance to
the charges of exaggeration often leveled against Dickens
— that in his fiction he reported the world very much as
he always saw it. Descriptions of scenes and events in his
letters sometimes sound exactly like passages of the
novels. There is, for example, a letter to Lady Burdett-
Coutts which reports his inspection of a slum area in the
Saint Mark's District of London, where she thought of
financing a housing project:

In one corner is a spot called Hickman's Folly (a Folly it is
much to be regretted that Hickman ever committed), which
looks like the last hopeless climax of everything poor and
filthy. There is a public house in it, with the odd sign of the
Ship Aground, but it is wonderfully appropriate, for everything seems to have got aground there — never to be got off
any more until the whole globe is stopped in its rolling and
shivered. No more roads than in an American swamp — odious sheds for horses, and donkeys, and vagrants, and rubbish,
in front of the parlor windows — wooden houses like horrible old packing cases full of fever for a countless number of
years. In a broken down gallery at the back of a row of these,
there was a wan child looking over at a starved old white
horse who was making a meal of oyster shells. The sun was
going down and flaring out like an angry fire at the child —

[30] "Family Names," *HW*, XV (30 May 1857), 525–28.

and the child, and I, and the pale horse, stared at one another
in silence for some five minutes as if we were so many figures
in a dismal allegory. I went round to look at the front of the
house, but the windows were all broken and the door was
shut up as tight as anything so dismantled could be. Lord
knows when anybody will go in to the child, but I suppose
it's looking over still — with a little wiry head of hair, as pale
as the horse, all sticking up on its head — and an old weazen
face — and two bony hands holding on the rail of the gallery,
with little fingers like convulsed skewers.[31]

This might well be a description of Tom-all-Alone's. It
is, in fact, part of an official report to a leading philan-
thropist of the day and the wealthiest woman in England,
telling her how to spend her money. This same conjunction of the observed world and the world of the novels
is perceptible in Dickens' macabre, comic description in
a letter to Wills of the row caused when an unfortunate
boy falls under the wheels of a wagon and is killed.[32]

In specific and detailed ways, too, Dickens bolsters his
imagination with facts. When he needs a harsh magistrate
for *Oliver Twist*, he arranges to be smuggled into court
to observe a notorious one.[33] In an item in his diary for
February 2, 1838, he reminds himself that the schoolmaster he had seen that day, while gathering material for
Nicholas Nickleby, had been convicted of gross neglect
of his boys, and that he must look the case up in the
newspapers.[34] In telling Lady Burdett-Coutts why he
plans to go to Switzerland for a while, he says he wants
to "get up some mountain knowledge in all the four

31 *Coutts Letters*, pp. 219–20.
32 *Letters* II, 553, 20 April 1854.
33 *Letters* I, 111, to Haines, 3 June 1837.
34 *Letters* I, 147.

seasons of the year, for purposes of fiction." [35] He has a
medical friend supply him with information on spontaneous combustion in human beings for *Bleak House*.[36] He
acquires some authentic circus slang to use in *Hard
Times*.[37] He always has his eye on the world around him
when he writes, but he sees from a special vantage, like
the man who spends the last night of the old year on top
of the Monument of Fish Street Hill in order to get a
perspective of the city.[38] The vantage, of course, is the
vantage of his own unique imagination. Santayana has
made the classic answer to the charge that this imagination is one that exaggerates, by attributing it to people
who have "no eyes and no ears," who "have only *notions*
of what things and people are" and "little sense for those
living grimaces that play from moment to moment upon
the countenance of the world." [39]

Though the sense of scene, and particularly the sense
of the London scene, is strong in Dickens' novels, the
world is pictured chiefly in terms of the individuals who
inhabit it. This emphasis is considered. An article on portrait painting in *All the Year Round* starts thus: "Portraits may be considered the highest effort of the painter's art." [40] Earlier, in *Household Words*, there had been
an eloquent essay on the face as an expression of the
human soul.[41] Dickens believed that an illustrator should
be able to take his cue from the text and that graphic

[35] *Letters* I, 747, to Lady Burdett-Coutts, 22 April 1846.
[36] *Letters* II, 446–47, to Elliotson, 7 February 1853.
[37] *Letters* II, 542–43, to Lemon, 20 February 1854.
[38] "All Night on the Monument," *HW*, XVII (30 January 1858),
145–48.
[39] "Dickens," in *Soliloquies in England* (London, 1922), pp. 65–66.
[40] "Portraits," *AYR*, XIV (19 August 1865), 91.
[41] "Faces," *HW*, X (16 September 1854), 97–101.

illustration need only be a kind of extension of the verbal illustration of character (and incident) found in the text.[42] He was at great pains to choose proper illustrators for his novels, and to see that the illustrators chosen worked closely from the verbal pictures he provided.[43] He could be tyrannical with his illustrators, as with other people, and at twenty-three spurred the far older and established Cruikshank to do his work both faster and more carefully.[44] He forced Seymour to follow the text of *The Pickwick Papers* for his illustrations with such ruthless insistence that Seymour's family and friends thought this a heavy contributing cause to his suicide.[45] Such a close connection between the character as described and the character as drawn would be possible only with as vivid a method of characterization as Dickens employed.

This vividness of characterization, which was part of his talent, also became a matter of literary principle. Commenting on some work submitted to him for criticism, he said: "You cannot interest your readers in any character unless you have first made them hate, or like him." [46] For physical vividness is only an adjunct to moral or spiritual vividness. E. M. Forster, dividing characterization roughly into two sorts, flat and round, cites

[42] A discussion of Doré argues that he, like Cruikshank or Hablot Browne, tried to render the dramatic portions of a book in his illustrations, whereas modern illustrators in general try to create a work of art independent of the book ("Book Illustrations," *AYR*, XVIII [10 August 1867], 151–55).

[43] His detailed correspondence with Marcus Stone, the illustrator of *Our Mutual Friend*, shows this well. This correspondence has not been published, but the letters themselves are part of the Dickens holdings of the Pierpont Morgan Library.

[44] See Johnson, p. 107.

[45] Johnson, pp. 166 ff. and 138.

[46] *Letters* I, 255, to Overs, 12 April 1840.

Dickens as one of the chief practitioners of the flat school. "Flat characters," he says, "were called 'humours' in the seventeenth century, and are sometimes called types, and sometimes caricatures. In their purest form, they are constructed round a single idea or quality: when there is more than one factor in them, we get the beginning of the curve towards the round." Of Dickens, he concludes that "his immense success with types suggests that there may be more in flatness than the severer critics admit." [47]

The consideration of the seventeenth-century concept of humors, particularly as it is employed by Ben Jonson, is useful and right. It is not insignificant that the first two plays Dickens produced when he started his ambitious amateur theatricals were *Every Man in His Humour* and *The Merry Wives of Windsor*. The dramatic nature of Dickens' characterization, however, is more general than this. Dickens was infatuated with the theater when he was a boy and tried to become an actor before he became a writer. [48] Accident or something deeper saved him for literature, but the dramatic impulse was partly absorbed into his novel-writing; [49] and the success with which his characterizations can be projected dramatically is attested to by the record of his dramatic readings and of the many plays and motion pictures derived from the novels.

His characterization surely goes more across the scale to roundness, also, than Forster allows. Pickwick, for example, is closer to the Falstaff of *Henry IV* than to the

[47] *Aspects of the Novel* (New York, 1927), pp. 103–12.
[48] Johnson, pp. 22–23 and 60–61.
[49] This speculation is developed by R. C. Churchill, among others, in "Dickens, Drama, and Tradition," *Scrutiny*, X (April 1942), 358–75.

Falstaff of *The Merry Wives*.[50] Dickens looked for something closer to verisimilitude in his characterization than is sometimes recognized. It worried him while he was at work on *Oliver Twist* that Fagin was "such an out and outer." [51] His comments on stories submitted for *Household Words* and *All the Year Round* are again helpful in showing his intent. To one aspirant author, he wrote: "The father is such a dolt, and the villain *such* a villain, the girl so exceptionally credulous and the means used to deceive them so very slight and transparent, that the reader *cannot* sympathize with their distresses . . . and the characters not being strongly marked (except in impossibilities) the Dialogues grow tedious and wearisome." [52] This distinction between extremity of character and markedness or vividness of character is important.

His view of character is reasonably related to his general view of the power of a meaningful story to be agreeable or amusing and to reveal its meaning of itself — which relates in turn to his faith in his audience and their capacity to understand a skillfully told story. To one author he complained that she did not let her characters "sufficiently work out their own purposes in dialogue and dramatic action." [53] He made a related complaint

---

[50] Note, too, how he reclaims Mrs. Gradgrind from flat type on her deathbed by reminding us that she is a human being like ourselves.

[51] *Letters* I, 173, to Forster, September 1838.

[52] *Letters* I, 229, to Overs, 27 September 1839.

[53] *Letters* II, 624, to Miss King, 9 February 1855. He told her also that the slanginess of one character, though not inaccurate, was nonetheless not right, because it was "the author's function to elevate such a characteristic, and soften it into something more expressive of the ardour and flush of youth, and its romance." This has obvious bearing on the often repeated complaint that Dickens' lower class characters speak as uneducated people could not speak. There is also an essay in *Household Words* on slang that emphasizes the undesirable features of the expansion of the language. ("Slang," VIII [24 September 1853], 73–78). See also the already cited Preface to *Oliver Twist*.

to Wills that a story they had was "all working machinery, and the people [were] not alive," so that the im-
probabilities obtruded as they would not if the story
were "so true and vivid, that the reader must accept it
whether he likes it or not." [54] The reader is continually
considered, that mass reader whom Dickens always has in
mind, as when he tells Percy Fitzgerald that though he
knows the disagreeableness of one of his characters is
intended, it "wants relief" nonetheless to take "the taste
of him, here and there, out of the reader's mouth." [55]

Dickens was opposed to severity of technique whether
in characterization or in narration. He cautioned Wilkie
Collins about telling a "story too severely," and advised
him to "mitigate the severity of your own sticking to it"
with "comicality," "whimsicality and humour." [56] Anticipation was for him a kind of severity, giving away
the outcome of the story too early and too surely, so that
all that remained to do was a very mechanical working-
out of what had already been made inevitable. A romantic, purportedly organic view of art underlies this: "I
think the business of art is to lay all that ground carefully, not with the care that conceals itself — to show,
by a backward light, what everything has been working
to — but only to *suggest*, until the fulfilment comes.
These are the ways of Providence, of which ways all art
is but a little imitation." [57] Much the same principle was
asserted when he answered Forster's objections to the
place of accident in *A Tale of Two Cities*, particularly
in regard to the death of Madame Defarge. "Where the
accident is inseparable from the passion and action of the

[54] *Letters* II, 653, 13 April 1855.
[55] *Letters* III, 393, 27 July 1864.
[56] *Letters* III, 282, 24 January 1862.
[57] *Letters* III, 125, to Collins, 6 October 1859.

character; where it is strictly consistent with the entire
design, and arises out of some culminating proceeding
on the part of the individual which the whole story has
led up to; it seems to me to become, as it were, an act
of divine justice." [58]

The objection to anticipation appears repeatedly. He
said of a story by Thomas Trollope that "he mars the
end by overanticipating it." [59] He suggested that Wilkie
Collins consider, in one of his stories, "the anticipation
contained in the last line or two of Norah's postscript." [60]
He told Wills that he had made a cut in the beginning
of a story accepted for *All the Year Round* because the
passage cut told the story before the story itself had even
fairly begun.[61] He wanted to leave in fiction some of
the interest of life itself — chance, surprise, unpredict-
ability, even within the necessary order of consequences.

He has related objections to giving the reader hints
and aids to his understanding that stem from a disbelief
in his intelligence. He warned Wilkie Collins that "the
great pains you take express themselves a trifle too much,
and you know that I always contest your disposition
to give an audience credit for nothing." He went on to
say that the three characters who tell the story in *The
Woman in White* "have a DISSECTIVE property in
common, which is essentially not theirs but yours; . . .
my own effort would be to strike more of what is got
that way out of them by collision with one another, and
by the working of the story." [62]

58 *Letters* III, 117, to Forster, August 1859. This is repeated in a letter
to Bulwer-Lytton, *Letters* III, 163, 5 June 1860.
59 *Letters* III, 303, to Wills, 14 September 1862.
60 *Letters* III, 309, 14 October 1862.
61 *Letters* III, 374, 20 December 1863.
62 *Letters* III, 145, 7 January 1860.

In three letters to Bulwer-Lytton,[63] though he was more deferential than with Collins, Dickens said much the same thing. He advised him not to feel that his audience needed help in order to understand him; if explanation was to be made, it should be made by one of the characters of the story speaking in his own person and not serving as a mere transparency for the author. To another contributor to *All the Year Round* he affirmed the same principle, that the people of her story should tell and act it, whereas she tended to tell it herself *"in a sort of impetuous breathless way."* The consequence of this, he said, was that too little was made of the events that actually are the story. In a passage very revealing of his own method as a novelist, he said:

Unless you really have led up to a great situation like Basil's death, you are bound in art to make more of it. Such a scene should form a chapter of itself. Impressed upon the reader's memory, it would go far to make the fortune of the book. Suppose yourself telling that affecting incident in a letter to a friend. Wouldn't you describe how you went through the life and stir of the streets and roads to the sick-room? Wouldn't you say what kind of room it was, what time of day it was, whether it was sunlight, starlight, or moonlight? Wouldn't you have a strong impression on your mind of how you were received, when you first met the look of the dying man, what strange contrasts were about you and struck you? [64]

One has only to think of the great death scenes in Dickens' novels to know that he is recommending his own practice.

Yet though Dickens was confident of the reader's abil-

[63] *Letters* III, 268, 18 December 1861; 269, 20 December 1861; 270, 25 December 1861.

[64] *Letters* III, 461–62, to Mrs. Brookfield, 20 February 1866.

ity to understand what was contained in a work of fiction, he also understood the difficulties of injecting the author's full intent into the work. There is in the author's mind a setting or context for what happens in a story that cannot be entirely present in the mind of any reader. Dickens knew this, as any writer of fiction is bound to come to know it. There are various ways to increase context and decrease the possible difference in intelligent understanding, however; and Dickens called the "introduced story" in the novels of Fielding and Smollett such a device, and he justified it because "it is sometimes really impossible to present, in a full book, the idea it contains (which yet it may be on all accounts desirable to present), without supposing the reader to be possessed of almost as much romantic allowance as would put him on a level with the writer." [65]

Dickens had great respect for craft and for originality. For the worn conventions that often stand for reality in art, he had rough contempt. *Household Words* published two attacks on the use of stock characters in fiction,[66] and one on the conventions of sentimental comedy, with examples taken from a mangled and pirated dramatic version of *Dombey and Son*.[67] This campaign was continued in *All the Year Round* with an article on the demise of the three-volume novel, with its machinery of elopements, duels, set phraseology and situations; [68] and a general spoofing of sensationalism in fiction and

[65] *Letters* II, 776, to Forster, 1856.
[66] "A Petition to the Novel-Writers," *HW*, XIV (6 December 1856), 481–85; "New Puppets for Old Ones," *HW*, XIX (29 January 1859), 210–12.
[67] "My Long Lost Chee-yld," *HW*, XVII (22 May 1858), 548–52.
[68] "Small-Beer Chronicles," *AYR*, IX (23 May 1863), 309–12.

drama which shows how far back in literary history some
of these conventions can be traced.[69]

Yet if the worn conventions do not make art, "life"
and "reality" do not make art either but must be
transformed into art. Dickens was very clear about this
and never underestimated its difficulty. Writing to a
would-be contributor to *Household Words*, he said: "I
need not say to *you*, that something more is wanted in
such a narrative, than its literal truth — that it is of the
very nature of such truths as are treated of here, to require to be told artistically, and with great discretion."[70]

A notice in the *Household Narrative* [71] of the publication of *Alton Locke* was scornful not only of Kingsley's
convictions but even more of his lack of skill as a novelist: "In English fiction, a semi-chartist novel called *Alton
Locke*, full of error and earnestness, and evidently by a
university man of the so-called Christian Socialist school,
is the most noticeable work of the kind that has lately
appeared." The balance between subject and art is suggested in a letter in which Dickens discusses *Uncle Tom's
Cabin*. "No doubt," he states, "a much lower art will
serve for the handling of such a subject in fiction, than
for a launch on the sea of imagination without such a
powerful bark." But he goes on nonetheless to point out
Mrs. Stowe's deficiencies as a novelist and, amusingly,
her borrowings from himself and Mrs. Gaskell.[72]

He detested lack of originality in any art. He was de-
pressed by most of the religious painting he saw in Italy
because he felt it showed a double slavishness, to the rules

---

[69] "Not a New 'Sensation,'" *AYR*, IX (25 July 1863), 517–20.
[70] *Letters* II, 236, to Tagart, 22 September 1850.
[71] *HN*, I (1850), 191.
[72] *Letters* II, 430–31, to Mrs. Watson, 22 November 1852.

of art and to the requirements of the church.[73] His re-
marks to Forster about the *Exposition universelle* held in
Paris in 1855 are particularly interesting in this regard.
He was appalled by the poverty of the English paintings
and more appalled when he compared them to the
French:

The general absence of ideas is horribly apparent . . . what we
know to be wanting in the men is wanting in their works —
character, fire, purpose, and the power of using the vehicle
and the model as mere means to an end. There is a horrid
respectability about most of the best of them — a little, finite,
systematic routine in them, strangely expressive to me of the
state of England itself. . . . There are no end of bad pictures
among the French, but, Lord! the goodness also! — the fear-
lessness of them; the bold drawing; the dashing conception;
the passion and action in them! [74]

Posterity has come largely to agree with his judgment
on the English painters of the mid-nineteenth century.
The French painters he does not mention by name; but
Baudelaire in his review of the exposition of 1855 [75] discusses Ingres and Delacroix, so the comparison should
have been depressing to any Englishman with a genuine
eye.

Like most artists, and with good enough reason, Dickens thought contemporary critics generally hostile to
originality. A burlesque piece in *Household Words* pur-
ported to show how a contemporary reviewer would review *Hamlet* if it were a new play; [76] and a similar article

[73] *Letters* I, 640, to Forster, 17 November 1844.
[74] *Letters* II, 700, to Forster, October 1855.
[75] *The Mirror of Art*, trans. Jonathan Mayne (New York, Anchor,
1956), pp. 203–19.
[76] "Something that Shakespeare Lost," *HW*, XV (17 January 1857),
49–52.

in *All the Year Round* attacked the tendency of critics to call anything original "sensational" and showed how one such critic would review *Macbeth* if it in turn were new.[77]

Dickens placed a high value also on that lesser order of originality — cleverness. He considered Wilkie Collins' *Hide and Seek* "the cleverest novel I have ever seen written by a new hand." [78] He detested the absence of cleverness — dullness. He constantly complained to Wills of the dullness of stories or articles they had accepted for *Household Words* or *All the Year Round*. A story by Miss Martineau was "heavy." [79] An entire number was heavy: "I doubt if anything so heavy (except stewed lead) could possibly be taken, before going to bed." [80] Another number was "gloomy," with Miss Martineau, again, "grimly bent upon the enlightenment of mankind," and Mrs. Gaskell's *North and South*, unsuccessfully divided into parts, "wearisome in the last degree." [81] He even complained of his favorite, Collins, finding the construction of *The Moonstone* "wearisome beyond endurance" and with "a vein of obstinate conceit in it that makes enemies of readers." [82]

---

[77] "The Sensational Williams," *AYR*, XI (13 February 1864), 14–17.

[78] *Letters* II, 570, to Georgina Hogarth, 25 July 1854. For a time Collins was singled out as his companion, crown prince, and heir apparent; and by 1862 Dickens was convinced that Collins would forge ahead of all the field, because he was "the only one who combined invention and power, both humorous and pathetic, with that invincible determination to work, and that profound conviction that nothing of worth is to be done without work, of which triflers and feigners have no conception" (*Letters* III, 304, to Collins, 20 September 1862).

[79] *Letters* II, 213, 29 March 1850.   [80] *Letters* II, 480, 5 August 1853.

[81] *Letters* II, 597–98, 14 October 1854. These lady writers, among the first contributors to *Household Words*, were also among its first troubles, because they required careful handling and pampering.

[82] *Letters* III, 660, 26 July 1868.

Dickens had, in addition to loftier criteria, the requirement of the professional writer that writing be competent and entertaining. He was bitterly against the "colorless, shapeless" bits of writing that "start up good subjects and get no kind of point or effect out of them. I would as soon dine off an old glove, as read such pale literary boiled veal." [83] After rewriting a story bought for *Household Words*, in order to make it presentable, he complained that it "would be as easy (almost) to write one, as I found it to get point and terseness out of such an infernal hash." [84] When he cut a story by Miss Martineau, he boasted that he had done it so "scientifically" that Miss Martineau would not be able to discover it.[85]

But technique and even originality, though always admired, had to be at the service of some serious purpose. For social concern was central to Dickens' mind and to his fiction. He was marvelously gratified when Meyerbeer said to him at a dinner party at the home of Lord John Russell: "Ah, mon ami illustre! que c'est noble de vous entendre parler d'haute voix morale, à la table d'un ministre!" [86] About this same time he wrote to a correspondent that "every day of my life I feel more and more that to be thoroughly in earnest is everything, and to be anything short of it is nothing." [87] He required this earnestness, this commitment, from art. When he wrote a short memorial on the death of Thackeray, he could not

[83] *Letters* II, 764, to Wills, 27 April 1856.
[84] *Letters* II, 350, to Wills, 9 October 1851.
[85] *Letters* II, 228, to Wills, 21 August 1850.
[86] See *Letters* II, 678, to Collins, 8 July 1855.
[87] *Letters* II, 712, to Morgan, *circa* November 1855.

even here exclude his belief that Thackeray's art was blemished by lapses in seriousness.[88]

This moral seriousness was a comparatively simple criterion for the young Dickens. He explained his dislike of Byron's poetry by saying: "It is not the province of a Poet to harp upon his own discontents, or to teach other people that they ought to be discontented." [89] He wrote to a man who, out of admiration for his writing, had named a son after him: "If I could ever learn that I had happily been the means of awakening within him any new love of his fellow-creatures . . . I should feel much pleasure from the knowledge." [90] Though the nature of his commitment as a writer darkened in time, the principles suggested by these two early statements did not essentially change. Seriousness, however, comes to mean more than the social seriousness it seemed too narrowly to mean to him at first. He is more aware of the place of artistic seriousness. It is true that one of the first writers eulogized in *Household Words* was the poet of the Corn Laws, Ebenezer Elliot; [91] but at about the same time, Dickens was impressing on contributors to *Household Words* his conviction that "literal truth" did not of itself constitute art, but required to be made art.[92]

The general burden of an essay on the art of fiction in *All the Year Round* in 1867 was, classically enough, that fiction is a way of organizing man's experience in

[88] "In Memoriam," *The Cornhill Magazine*, IX (February 1864), 129–32.
[89] *Letters* I, 279, to Harford, 25 November 1840.
[90] *Letters* I, 456, to Hughes, 17 May 1842.
[91] "Ebenezer Elliott," *HW*, I (22 June 1850), 310–12.
[92] *Letters* II, 236, to Tagart, 22 September 1850.

the world so that he can comprehend it;[93] and a few years earlier there had been an article on the artist John Leech in which Leech was praised because he held "a mirror up to the time."[94] These statements are at a low enough key of originality, but it must be remembered that they are pitched toward a popular audience of about 300,000. To Dickens, a writer seemed to have no function without a large audience; and writing to the actor Macready of "the eternal duties of the arts to the people," he said: "The more we see of life and its brevity, and the world and its varieties, the more we know that no exercise of our abilities in any art, but the addressing of it to the great ocean of humanity in which we are drops, and not to bye-ponds (very stagnant) here and there, ever can or ever will lay the foundations of an endurable retrospect."[95] Of his *Child's History of England*, closer to the discipline of fiction than to any conventional discipline of history, he said: "It is my hope, by presenting the truth in an agreeable and winning form, to lead young people to . . . pursue it further."[96]

Purpose seemed to him a necessary and major part of any work of fiction. It could be one of the prime things that made a story work. Thus it is the "fine plain purpose," controlled by literary competence, that he admires in the work of Harriet Martineau[97] and the lack of purpose in another writer that makes agreeable technique futile.[98] His great admiration for *The Vicar of*

[93] "The Spirit of Fiction," *AYR*, XVIII (27 July 1867), 118–20.
[94] "Mr. Leech's Gallery," *AYR*, VII (5 July 1862), 390–94.
[95] *Letters* II, 444, 14 January 1853.
[96] *Letters* II, 443, to Staples, 5 January 1853.
[97] *Letters* II, 428, to Wills, November 1852.
[98] *Letters* II, 401–02, to Young, 21 July 1852.

Wakefield rested on his belief that it was a "book of which I think it is not too much to say that it has perhaps done more good in the world, and instructed more kinds of people in virtue, than any other fiction ever written." [99] For his own fiction, Dickens had similar hopes. With *The Chimes*, for example, he wished to make "a great blow for the poor. Something powerful, I think I can do, but I want to be tender too, and cheerful . . . and if my design be anything at all, it has a grip upon the very throat of the time." [100] He told Carlyle, to whom the book was dedicated, that he hoped *Hard Times* would "shake some people in a terrible mistake of these days." [101] When a reviewer suggested that this novel was about a strike at Preston which had been reported in *Household Words*, Dickens called this a mistake that did a double disservice: it gave people a false idea of how novels were written, and "it localizes (so far as your readers are concerned) a story which has a direct purpose in reference to the working people all over England." [102]

Dickens posits an order of responsibility for the writer: to grasp his readers as he can, but then not let them get away until they have been led to see the truth. The second is not possible without the first, but he was notably impatient with the artist who, having a hold on his audience, failed to exploit this opportunity to demonstrate the truth. With Prescott's *The Conquest of Mexico*, which he admired, he had nonetheless this curious fault to find:

[99] *Coutts Letters*, p. 144.
[100] *Letters* I, 627, to Forster, 8 October 1844.
[101] *Letters* II, 567, 13 July 1854.
[102] *Letters* II, 546, to Cunningham, 11 March 1854.

I only wonder that, having such an opportunity of illustrating the doctrine of visible judgments, he never remarks, when Cortes and his men tumble the idols down the temple steps and call upon the people below to take notice that their gods are powerless to help themselves, that possibly, if some intelligent native had tumbled down the image of the Virgin or patron saint after them, nothing very remarkable might have ensued in consequence.[103]

It is a cranky and special truth he asks of Prescott, and possibly not Prescott's truth at all, but it shows how Dickens expected an artist to work and how he tried himself to work.

He confides to Forster a similar, but more serious, quarrel with *The Bottle,* Cruikshank's portrayal of the ravages of alcohol:

The philosophy of the thing, as a great lesson, I think all wrong; because to be striking, and original too, the drinking should have begun in sorrow, or poverty, or ignorance — the three things in which, in its awful aspect, it *does* begin. The design would then have been a doublehanded sword — but too "radical" for good old George, I suppose.[104]

Again it is "the truth" he wants and does not find here, and it is manifest that no inherent truth would satisfy him — he requires assertion. Thus one of the two moments that struck him most in a performance of the play *Thirty Years of a Gambler's Life* came when the gambler, having been charged by his friend with murder, "suddenly went headlong mad and took him by the

103 *Letters* I, 554, to Felton, 2 January 1844.
104 *Letters* II, 52, 2 September 1847.

throat and howled out, 'It wasn't I who murdered him —
it was Misery!' " [105]

This insistence on "truth" was most apparent in the
1840's, when Dickens was still in many ways allied with
the Reform movement and had a more present belief in
improvement than he could later manage. Yet even when
he became less optimistic, he did not lose his belief in
the capacity of art to affect people's lives. An article in
Household Words in 1858 finds a challenge to writers
in the fact that the penny journals have an audience of
three million readers who know nothing of good or intelligent writing.[106] The onus is put not on the public which
reads trash but on the writers who do not contrive some
way to lead the public to something better.

When the traces of a theory have been gathered, it is
clear why Dickens made so few extended statements of
literary principle. To compare his prefaces with James's
prefaces, for example, is to show the paucity of his literary principles and their relative lack of complexity. But
this deficiency is poverty only when we regard the
aesthetic apart from the work it reflects or rationalizes.
For on his own meagre aesthetic, Dickens was able to
found as rich a body of fiction as has been created by
any writer in English.

James's literary theory sheds light — and some obscurity too — in all directions. Dickens' statements are
apologetics really — to use the term descriptively, not
pejoratively — illuminating little but his own practice, and
even this only in gross. This they do considerably, however, showing the special objects and requirements he

[105] *Letters* II, 632, to Forster, February 1855.
[106] "The Unknown Public," *HW*, XVIII (21 August 1858), 217–22.

set himself, as a highly inventive, productive, and original writer who meant his novels to be read avidly by a huge audience for whom he felt an intense tenderness and concern, and whose lives he hoped his fiction would serve to better.

Chapter Two

THE SOCIAL AND POLITICAL ISSUES

In Dickens' novels, characters are cast in detailed and purposeful social situations, and an evaluated social world is created. Yet even those critics who agree roughly that this is so, and agree further on the stature of these novels, disagree markedly as to Dickens' own politics and view of society — disagree in fundamental respects, that is, on what disposition of mind lies behind and shapes these novels. Sometimes the disagreement has to do with personal conviction. G. K. Chesterton, a Catholic with mixed politics of his own, bolsters as he can Dickens' orthodoxy.[1] T. A. Jackson, a Marxist whose genuine insight is marred by insufficient respect for brute fact, attempts to show that Dickens was a Communist in all but name, and "that the really fundamental incompatibility between Dickens and his wife lay in the complete antithesis of their convictions about contemporary society as a whole." [2]

The problem remains even when there is no personal bias. The best modern critics of Dickens have described

[1] *Charles Dickens: A Critical Study* (New York, 1906).
[2] *Charles Dickens: The Progress of a Radical* (New York, 1938), p. 201.

an enigmatic mixture of radicalism and conservatism in his novels, and tried, with varying results, to find a common-sense rationale for the mixture.[3] Common sense, however, is an insufficient bulwark against purposeful misinterpretation, and now, as conservatism becomes the mode, there is a tendency to refashion Dickens also, and to make him seem safer than he was. One recent writer says that Dickens finds his solution in philanthropy, not government; that he looks to the past instead of the future; that when he "describes a wicked rich man he is portraying a moral type and not a class type."[4] Does this come to fair terms with the matter? For Dickens found in fact no social cure-all in either philanthropy or government. He looked more to the past than to the future when he wrote, because there was more there to see and describe; yet he had no morbid fear of the future, and defended industrialism and progress to his more reactionary contemporaries. Increasingly, too, he was aware of, and in his fiction took sharp cognizance of the place of class in the formation of character.

Our knowledge of Dickens' politics and view of society can be given more specific content if we are willing to abandon, at least initially, the terms "liberal," "radical," and "conservative," as we understand them, and then to give detailed consideration to the views found in Dickens' letters and in the more than one thousand issues of *Household Words*, *The Household Narrative*, and *All the Year Round* he edited, and for which he frequently wrote, during the last twenty years of his life.

[3] Wilson, for example; or George Orwell, "Charles Dickens," in *Dickens, Dali, and Others* (New York, 1946), pp. 1–75.

[4] William O. Aydelotte, "The England of Marx and Mills as Reflected in Fiction," *Jour. of Econ. Hist.*, Suppl. VIII (1948), 42–58.

The views expressed in these magazines conform to Dickens' own views even when they are not from his pen, for he was a dictatorial editor — or "Conductor," as he significantly called himself. At one time he published the following avowal of responsibility: "The statements and opinions of this Journal generally are, of course, to be received as the statements and opinions of its Conductor." [5] The closeness of his supervision of these magazines and the opinions they encouraged is attested to by his correspondence with his sub-editor, W. H. Wills.[6]

[5] "Note," *AYR*, X (26 December 1863), 419.

[6] In the *Letters*, there are 203 letters to Wills in the period 1850–70, when Dickens was conducting the magazines. This number gains proportion when we realize that by and large Dickens wrote to Wills only when one or the other of them was not in the London area, and they could not do business in person. In this same period of twenty years, there are only 39 letters to Macready, 76 to Bulwer-Lytton, and even to Forster, just 194.

Of course the significance of these figures is affected by the accidents governing which letters have survived and which have not, and may be changed when the new edition of Dickens' letters now being prepared is published. But a sampling of the letters to Wills in 1854 — a critical year in my argument — shows something of the specific nature of Dickens' conductorship. 20 April: "I have gone very carefully over the whole No. . . . It is a very good one, I think, and I see no occasion to alter the course of the making-up, or to change any paper" (II, 553). 14 July (from Boulogne): "The C. P. by R. S. [probably an article on the Crystal Palace] is very well done, but I cannot make up my mind to lend my blow to the great Forge-bellows of puffery at work. I so heartily desire to have nothing to do with it, that I wish you would cancel this article altogether, and substitute something else. As to the guidebooks, I think they are a sufficiently flatulent botheration in themselves, without being discussed. A lurking desire is always upon me to put Mr. Laing's speech on Accidents to the public, as Chairman of the Brighton Railway, against his pretensions as a chairman of public Instructors and guardians. And I don't know but what I may come to it at some odd time. This strengthens me in my wish to avoid the bellows" (p. 568). 2 Aug. (from Boulogne): "Manage the proofs of H. W. so that I may not have to correct them on a Sunday. I am not going over to the Sabbatarians, but like the haystack (particularly) on a Sunday morning" (p. 574). 25 Sept. (from Boulogne): He complains that an issue is too

The attempt has been too much, or too nearly exclusively, to derive Dickens' politics from his novels. The logic of this is of course clear: it is the novels in which we are primarily interested. But the basis of difficulty then is equally clear: the novel is a work of art, serving complex and multiple intentions, and not an expression of opinion. Had Dickens not known this well, he would never have been a great novelist. Yet he meant his novels to be serious, even earnest, and social concern was basic to his own gravity. The nature of this social concern can be got at most usefully and specifically in terms of the subjects Dickens himself most often expressed himself about: representative government; class structure and English society; the poor, the poor laws, charity and self-sufficiency; money and speculation, industry and progress.

Dickens' view of representative government, sceptical from the first, becomes more severe in the mid-fifties. In 1850 he still felt that representative government could be improved, and could be the instrument for dealing with Britain's needs. *The Household Narrative* in

---

frivolous, and asks that something be pulled out of it to make room for his own "To Working Men," a strong piece (p. 589). In another letter from Boulogne he tells Wills to report on a meeting of manufacturers at Manchester "with a view to the prevention of Boiler explosions, and their consequent injuries to workpeople." He wants this reported in fairness to the manufacturers, because he has been attacking them for their negligence in safety matters (pp. 592–93). 14 Oct. (from Boulogne): "I have taken out that passage about paper instantly rising 20 per cent if the Newspaper Stamp were taken off, for I think it a hazardous assumption to broach so very positively" (p. 597). He also objects to certain remarks offensive to the French in this issue. In other letters to Wills, quoted later in this article, there are similar illuminations of Dickens' editorial practice.

that year attacked the property requirement for the franchise; [7] and *Household Words* in that year and the next carried two attacks on government inefficiency, one on the problem that was even then referred to as red tape, and another on the peculiar *chinoiserie* of investigating commissions.[8] The satire of these articles aims to stimulate reform, not subversion. The distinction is important, for much of Dickens' later work is precisely subversive.

Dickens carried away from his early experience as a Parliamentary reporter a very low opinion of the House of Commons. In 1851 he gave instructions for a series of false book shelves with humorous titles to be painted over a panel in the library of his house in London, and the final title on the list of titles he supplied the carpenter was "Hansard's Guide to Refreshing Sleep. As many volumes as possible." [9] A few years later he wished "to have . . . every man in England feel something of the contempt for the House of Commons that I have." [10] His contempt was still, however, for a redeemable body. *Household Words* issued a call to workingmen advising them to insist on their right to decent, sanitary housing, and to direct their demands to Parliament, which could give them what they needed in one session, if it so desired.[11] This article was strong and inflammatory, but

[7] *HN*, I (March 1850), 51.

[8] "Red Tape," *HW*, II (15 February 1851), 481–84; "The Royal Rotten Row Commission," *HW*, I (15 June 1850), 274–76.

[9] *Letters* II, 354, to Eeles, 22 Oct. Of course this is an ironic comment on Hansard's parliamentary reports.

[10] *Letters* II, 585, to Forster, September 1854.

[11] "To Working Men," *HW*, X (7 October 1854), 169–70. This article was written by Dickens, and he defended it to a frightened friend by saying that the Government "will never do these things . . . until

talked only of what was considered possible within the given frame of government.

But in the following year, 1855, Dickens begins to talk more and more of the distance between the government and the real life and needs of the people. *Household Words* has an article on public ignorance of the mismanagement and corruption in government and big business; [12] and in a letter to Forster, Dickens says: "I am hourly strengthened in my belief that our political aristocracy and our tuft-hunting are the death of England. In all this business I don't see a gleam of hope. As to the popular spirit, it has come to be so entirely separated from the Parliament and Government, and so perfectly apathetic about them both, that I seriously think it a most portentous sign." [13] *Household Words* continues to operate as though the distance were bridgeable. It prints an attack on the tendency of the government and the ruling classes to treat the people as an irresponsible group of infants, and a plea for an honest examination of the entire state of government in England.[14] But writing again to Forster, Dickens once more pronounces representative government "altogether a failure with us," with the people rendered "unfit for it" by "the English gentilities and subserviences"; "the whole thing," he says, "has

---

they are made election questions and the working-people unite to express their determination to have them, or to keep out of Parliament by every means in their power, every man who turns his back upon these first necessities" (*Coutts Letters*, p. 273). Health and sanitation are perhaps the most characteristic grounds for his insistence on the need for change.

[12] "That Other Public," *HW*, XI (3 February), 1–4.

[13] *Letters* II, 622, 3 February 1855.

[14] "The Great Baby," XII (4 August), 1–4, ascribed to Dickens in Kitton; "Our Commission," XII (11 August), 25–27.

broken down since that great seventeenth-century time." [15]

To the actor and stage manager Macready, he wrote in the same tone but in more detail:

As to the suffrage, I have lost hope even in the ballot. We appear to me to have proved the failure of representative institutions without an educated and advanced people to support them. What with teaching people to "keep in their stations," what with bringing up the soul and body of the land to be a good child, or to go to the beer-shop, to go a-poaching and go to the devil; what with having no such thing as a middle class (for though we are perpetually bragging of it as our safety, it is nothing but a poor fringe on the mantle of the upper); what with flunkyism, toadyism, letting the most contemptible lords come in for all manner of places, reading The Court Circular for the New Testament, I do reluctantly believe that the English people are habitually consenting parties to the miserable imbecility into which we have fallen, *and never will help themselves out of it*. Who is to do it, if anybody is, God knows. But at present we are on the down-hill road to being conquered, and the people WILL be content to bear it, sing "Rule Britania," and WILL NOT be saved.[16]

This lack of concern with the major issue of reform, extension of the suffrage, and the related lack of faith in the middle class show the extent of Dickens' despair.

Still, *Household Words* continues, though with less frequency, to present the needs for reform. Significantly, however, broad social and governmental issues rather

---

[15] *Letters* II, 693, 30 September 1855. With "that great seventeenth-century time," Dickens is most likely referring to Cromwell, his admiration for whom he testifies to in his *Child's History of England*. Cromwell represented for him a kind of virile republicanism in the most marked contrast to the weak subservience he felt in the social and political life of his own time.

[16] *Letters* II, 695, 4 October 1855.

than immediate political issues are treated. There is a piece on the need to revise, codify, and rationalize British law; and there is another attack on red tape and futile legislation.[17] The comparative hopefulness of these articles reflects Dickens' sense of his public responsibilities as the proprietor of a magazine with mammoth circulation and influence,[18] and his fear of hastening England toward the violence he saw as coming. It does not represent any retreat from the extremity of his view of the country's situation, which continues to be plain in his correspondence.

In March of 1857 he declared the House of Commons "to be getting worse every day," and "representative Government . . . a miserable failure among us," with the people at Westminster engaged in party squabbles while the real troubles of the country were visible "within a few yards." When he was asked to stand for an uncontested seat in the House of Commons, he refused as he had done several times before and was to do several times again, saying he could "be far more useful and far more independent in my own calling than in the House of Commons and . . . no consideration would induce me to become a Member of that amazing institution." [19] He believed that representative government in England

17 "Law and Order," *HW*, XIII (29 March 1856), 241–45. (This plea recurs twice in 1863: "Consolidate the Statutes!" *AYR*, IX [1 Aug. 1863], 543–49; "Patched Law," *AYR*, IX [22 Aug. 1863], 606–09). "Flowers of British Legislation," *HW*, XIII (7 June 1856), 490–93.

18 *Household Words* sold as many as 40,000 copies a week, and its successor *All the Year Round* reached a circulation of 300,000 weekly (see Johnson, pp. 946–47) and for a time exceeded the circulation of the *Times* (Johnson, p. 995).

19 *Letters* II, 838, to Paxton, 1 March; II, 839–40, to de la Prynne, 14 March 1857.

reached its nadir under Palmerston, "a man notoriously of no conviction and no sentiment," and "holding the dead bones of an old office that has got to be rotten," and felt literature "to be made for better uses" than constructing polite mitigations for the true state of affairs.[20]

The railway accident at Staplehurst on 9 June 1865, in which Dickens was very nearly killed and the trauma of which he bore for the rest of his life, became for him the prime example of the sort of thing that the corruptness of the government made inevitable. "I think more and more what an ill-governed country this is, and what a pass our political system has got to. Here has this enormous railway No-System grown up without guidance, and now its abuses are so represented in Parliament by Directors, contractors, scrip jobbers, and so forth, that no minister dare touch it." Again, a few months later, he cited the state of affairs in India and the lack of any proper control of the railroads as prime evidences of the British government's ineffectuality.[21]

In the last five years of his life, a testy sense of personal affront comes into his remarks. In one of his letters he makes interesting clarification of a public statement that was misrepresented in the press: "My faith in the people governing is on the whole infinitesimal; my faith in The People governed, is, on the whole, illimitable." [22] And

20 *Letters* III, 232, to Morley, 28 Aug. 1861. Earlier he had said: "I have never doubted Lord Palmerston to be (considering the age in which he lives) the emptiest impostor and the most dangerous delusion, ever known" (*Coutts Letters*, p. 326).

21 *Letters* III, 430, to Bulwer-Lytton, 6 July; III, 446, to de Cerjat, 30 November.

22 *Letters* III, 751, to Chamberlain, 17 Nov. 1869. This is nearly a classic statement. G. M. Trevelyan says of Robert Owen, e.g., that he, "despairing of the governors, turned to the governed." *British History*

a few months before he died he wrote to Lord Lytton: "Indeed, I suppose in the main that there is very little difference between our opinions. I do not think the present Government worse than another, and I think it better than another by the presence of Mr. Gladstone; but it appears to me that our system fails." [23] This is the dejection of a man who sees life bound in the rigor mortis of an old dead system, yet cannot reconcile himself to any violent breaking free. But such a combination of radicalism and conservatism need not seem enigmatic. No one who has any attachment to place, people, ways of life, can feel simply destructive about them no matter to what bad end they are moving; and part of the necessity for passion in any radicalism is the need to overcome personal reluctance as well as obdurate status itself.

Dickens shows little familiarity with the work of any social thinkers of his day aside from Carlyle [24] and Bentham. He was not a great reader, and the enormous activity of his life scarcely left time for reading; but he knew and saw much of men who were readers and students, and might through them have become acquainted with the ideas of such works as *The Communist Manifesto* (1848) or Friedrich Engels' *Condition of the Working Class in England in 1844* (1845). There seem to be no

---

in the Nineteenth Century and After, rev. ed. (London, 1937), p. 185. Beyond this, Owen's and Dickens' careers are a study in difference or contrast.

[23] *Letters* III, 763, 14 Feb. 1870.

[24] Carlyle he knew personally, admired, resembled and differed from, and had certainly read to some extent. For a consideration of their personal and intellectual relations, see Mildred G. Christian, "Carlyle's Influence Upon the Social Theory of Dickens," *The Trollopian*, I, iv (March 1947), 27–35; II, i (June 1947), 11–26.

references to either Marx or Engels in Dickens' writings, however, and there is no particular evidence that they had any influence on his thought.

Much of what Dickens learned, though, he learned in his early life, from his experience and from his reading, and the circumstances of his childhood could hardly have allowed even a less perceptive child to escape some of the meaning of class difference. Nor would his reading in Fielding, Smollett, and Goldsmith have hindered a class consciousness. In *The Pickwick Papers* class is used much as it is used by the earlier novelists. But in Dickens' later novels, though this use is not abandoned, another less neutral view of class also emerges.

Nothing has been more emphasized by Dickens' biographers than his sense in his childhood and early manhood of being in a disadvantageous situation vis-à-vis "good society." With success and lionization came the chance to recoup. But he did not move into high places with any simple relief of acceptance. Quite consciously he took tokens of restitution for what had formerly been denied him; and he was vengeful and disagreeable whenever he felt his pride or status at all crowded.[25] This attitude involves more, however, than feelings of personal wrong. Very early he saw the entire social structure as an ignorant sham. "I declare I never go into what is called 'society' [but] that I am aweary of it, despise it, hate it, and reject it. The more I see of its extraordinary conceit, and its stupendous ignorance of what is passing out of doors, the more certain I am that

[25] See, for an extreme example, Dickens' account to Forster of refusing to appear before Queen Victoria in costume between the acts of *The Frozen Deep: Letters* II, 859, 5 July 1857.

it is approaching the period when, being incapable of
reforming itself, it will have to submit to be reformed
by others off the face of the earth." [26] But his sense of
social difference did not yet include any belief in a difference of class interests. Even six years later, for example,
he attacked the notion that there was a laboring class
with its own distinct interests.[27]

Social pretense and the ignorance and incapacities it
fosters are what he saw first, and *Household Words* hit
at these in a variety of ways: it satirized snobbery in
schools; it found that the concept of "gentleman" had
deteriorated to mere superficialities; it scoffed at the
foolishness and impermanence of fashion; it examined
idiocy caused by inbreeding as an example of the snobbery of the best families.[28] In the latter part of 1854, a
new note of warning comes into Dickens' statements.
Writing to Lady Burdett-Coutts of the government's failure to take proper measures against the cholera epidemic,
he warned that in time the people, advancing in their
knowledge of what could be done, would not stand for
such negligence; and that two more epidemics would
bring on "such a shake in this country as never was seen
on Earth since Sampson pulled the Temple down upon
his head." [29] This threat of revolution is very much in
Dickens' mind hereafter as something he both anticipates
and dreads. In these matters as in others, 1855 is Dickens'
crucial year. The increasing misery of his personal life

---

[26] *Letters* I, 588–89, to Forster, March 1844.
[27] *HN*, I (March 1850), 51.
[28] "A Free (and Easy) School," IV (15 Nov. 1851), 169–73; "Gentlemen in History," VII (25 June 1853), 394–96; "Fashion," VIII (29 Oct.
1853), 193–96; "Idiots Again," IX (15 April 1854), 197–200.
[29] *Coutts Letters*, p. 273.

as his marriage neared an end had something to do with
his despair. But this does not invalidate his judgment
of what was happening in the world around him; indeed,
he was likely to have some of his deepest perceptions
about his society when personal troubles had torn away
many of the buffers that lay between himself and that
society.

That the disastrous disclosures of Sebastopol should
lead to the appointment of Palmerston as Prime Minister
seemed to him a supreme failure in crisis. He spoke again
of his fear of revolution:

There is nothing in the present time at once so galling and
so alarming to me as the alienation of the people from their
own public affairs. . . . And I believe the discontent to be
so much the worse for smouldering instead of blazing openly,
that it is extremely like the general mind of France before
the breaking out of the first Revolution, and is in danger of
being turned by any one of a thousand accidents . . . into such
a devil of a conflagration as never has been beheld since.

Meanwhile, all our English tuft-hunting, toad-eating, and
other manifestations of accursed gentility . . . ARE expressing
themselves every day. So, every day, the disgusted millions
with this unnatural gloom and calm upon them are confirmed
and hardened in the very worst of moods. Finally, round all
this is an atmosphere of poverty, hunger, and ignorant despera-
tion, of the mere existence of which, perhaps not one man in
a thousand of those not actually enveloped in it, through the
whole extent of the country, has the least idea.[30]

To his ponderous and conservative friend John Forster
he is more shy with his Cassandra cries, merely describ-

[30] *Letters* II, 651–52, to Layard, 10 April 1855.

ing the "prospect" as "deplorable." [31] But with Lady
Burdett-Coutts he is open with his fears, and links them
strongly to his view of reform: "The people will not
bear for any length of time what they bear now. I see
it clearly written in every truthful indication that I am
capable of discerning anywhere. And I want to interpose
something between them and their wrath. For this reason
solely, I am a Reformer heart and soul." [32] Writing to
her again of some judgment she had passed on Austen
Henry Layard, evidently accusing him of provoking unrest, he says: "I differ from you altogether, as to his
setting class against class. He finds them already set in
opposition. And I think you hardly bear in mind that as
there are two great classes looking at each other in this
question, so there are two sides to the question itself.
You assume that the popular class take the initiative. Now
as *I* read the story, the aristocratic class did that, years
and years ago, and it is *they* who have put *their* class in
opposition to the country — not the country which puts
itself in opposition to *them*." [33] It is clear here that
Dickens no longer thinks of the middle class as a figur-
ing entity, but only, as he soon puts it, "a poor fringe on
the mantle of the upper," [34] and that he sees for the opposition between the two remaining classes no easy dissolution. Six weeks later he tells Lady Burdett-Coutts
that the riots in Hyde Park against the Sunday Bill,
which restricted the amusements of the populace on the

[31] *Letters* II, 655, 27 April 1855.
[32] *Coutts Letters*, p. 298.
[33] *Coutts Letters*, p. 299. Layard was the archeologist and excavator
of Nineveh, whose political convictions had finally led him into Commons and an active but futile political life.
[34] *Letters* II, 695, to Macready, 4 October 1855.

Sabbath, were an indication of the kind of violence continued Parliamentary ignorance of the state of the people might bring about.[35]

The new and foreboding belief in class opposition makes class a shaping and motivating element in Dickens' later novels. Edmund Wilson finds it Dickens' purpose in all his novels to make real to the governing class the people they govern, who are unreal for them, "who figure for Parliament as strategical counters and for Political Economy as statistics." [36] But by the fifties, or at least by 1855, Dickens had lost most of his belief that anything could make the poor real to the aristocrats and their "poor fringe." The change is, of course, in strategy, not sympathy.

In late 1853, *Household Words* had printed an account of the lengthy strike of the cotton workers at Preston, contending that the only cause of the prolongation of the strike was misunderstanding based on ignorance of common interest. In January 1854, Dickens went himself to Preston and on the train met a man who insisted that the strikers "wanted to be ground," "to bring 'em to their senses," and scoffed at Dickens' assertion that understanding could settle the trouble.[37] But in the two years after his comments on the strike at Preston, Dickens' ideas about the strike as an instrument of industrial relations showed a significant change. Henry Morley, a regular contributor to *Household Words*, wrote an acaacount of another strike for the magazine, and when Dickens sent the proof of the article back to Wills, he

[35] *Letters* II, 674, 27 June 1855.
[36] "The Two Scrooges," p. 26.
[37] "Locked Out," VIII (10 Dec.), 345-48. See Johnson, pp. 795-96; also, "On Strike," *HW*, VIII (11 Feb. 1854), 553-59.

indicated the changes that had to be made before the article could be published:

I cannot represent myself as holding the opinion that all strikes among this unhappy class of society who find it so difficult to get a peaceful hearing, are always necessarily wrong; because I don't think so. . . . Shew them to be in the wrong here, but in the name of the Eternal Heavens shew only upon the merits of this question. Nor can I possibly adopt the representation that these men are wrong because, by throwing themselves out of work, they throw other people, possibly without their consent. If such a principle had anything in it, there would have been no civil war; no raising by Hampden of a troop of Horse, to the detriment of Buckinghamshire Agriculture; no self sacrifice in the political world. And O Good God when Morley treats of the suffering of wife and children, can he suppose that these mistaken men don't feel it in the depths of their hearts, and don't honestly and honourably — most devoutly and faithfully — believe — that for those very children when they shall have children, they are bearing all these miseries now! [38]

He had come now to see the strike as a desperate instrument for those who had no other means available to them; and a couple of years later an article in *Household Words* was to suggest that a consumers' strike might also be an effective social weapon.[39]

Though *Household Words* continued mostly to hammer away at problems like snobbery,[40] in his own mind

[38] *Letters* II, 721-22, 6 Jan. 1856. The terms in which he insists on the changes — "represent myself," "adopt the representation" — show why any opinion voiced in *Household Words* can be pretty surely considered Dickens' own opinion.

[39] "Strike!" XVII (6 Feb. 1858), 169-72.

[40] "The Toady Tree," XI (26 May 1855), 385-87; "Family Names," XV, (30 May 1857), 525-28.

Dickens was concerned with more extreme matters. "Nobody knows," he said, "what the English people will be when they wake up at last." [41] Failures in patriotism among the people did not surprise him, and he became "demoniacal" when he thought how the English "suffered a system to go on which has blighted generous ambition, and put reward out of the common man's reach." [42]

At times, the tone of *Household Words* and its successor, *All the Year Round*, became more extreme too, even while circulation was increasing. In 1861 *All the Year Round* published a piece called "On the Civil War Now Raging in England," an account of the state of England in Hobbesian terms, as a war of each against all, going beyond class war to a total anarchy of individual struggle or jungle existence.[43] This is an image of surface appearance, however. Beneath this surface Dickens continued for the rest of his life to see the opposition of the two great classes, with the aristocrats the aggressors, and the popular class becoming aggressive finally only after long abuse and in self-defense.

Dickens learned about poverty in the least desirable way, by being a poor child. His interest in the poor thereafter was constant and passionate. The pity and the pain of their condition were always apparent to him, and part of the great obsessive center of his writing. In all his fiction, there was purpose in his portraits of the poor: "I have great faith in the Poor; to the best of my ability

[41] *Coutts Letters,* p. 326.
[42] *Letters* II, 889, to Lady Burdett-Coutts, 4 October 1857.
[43] *AYR,* V (17 August 1861), 489–92.

I always endeavour to present them in a favourable light to the rich; and I shall never cease, I hope, until I die, to advocate their being made as happy and as wise as the circumstances of their condition in its utmost improvement, will admit of their becoming." [44] The "circumstances of their condition" ranged wide in his mind. He defended vanity and color in poor women's dress to Lady Burdett-Coutts as one of "the good influences of a poor man's house." [45] He opposed the Sunday Law because he thought it discriminated against the amusements of the poor, and regretted the elimination of village sports and of shooting for the average farmer or villager for similar reasons.[46] He believed that some measures meant to help the poor would in fact do the reverse, and that the proposal of such measures showed an ignorance of the actual circumstances of the lives of the poor. Thus he refused in 1843 to support factory legislation to reduce the length of the working day, because he thought the poor could not afford the loss of income that would attend the shorter working day.[47]

He had no soft ideas of the blessings of poverty, and the poor often seemed disgusting to him, particularly if they happened not to be the English poor. The dregs of the population of Naples he described to Forster as "mere squalid, abject, miserable animals for vermin to batten on; slouching, slinking, ugly, shabby, scavenging scarecrows." [48] His long, often virtually daily correspond-

[44] *Letters* I, 589-90, to Staples, 3 April 1844.
[45] *Coutts Letters*, pp. 338-39.
[46] This occurs in many places, but a good example is "Pinchback's Amusements," *AYR*, VII (29 March 1862), 71-72.
[47] *Letters* I, 505, to Smith, 1 February.
[48] *Letters* I, 658, 11 February 1845.

ence with Lady Burdett-Coutts in regard to her reform
home for prostitutes at Shepherd's Bush also shows this
combination of concern and hard practicality, and at
times distaste. He habitually linked poverty with filth
and disease, and the connections between poverty, sanitation, and disease provide perhaps the most exploited
subject in both *Household Words* and *All the Year
Round*.[49] Crime, too, he sees as a product of poverty and
its companion, ignorance.[50] *Household Words* and *All
the Year Round* are used repeatedly to publicize certain
specific conditions of the poor, as well as their general
plight. Typical subjects dealt with are inadequate housing and attempts to improve it, or conditions of women
employed in factories, and how this contrasts with the
conditions of women still working in home or cottage
industries.[51]

In the last twenty years of his life, one of Dickens'
chief blows for the poor was his opposition to the Poor
Law of 1834. Even in 1842 he had written: "Pray tell
Mr. Chadwick [52] . . . I *do* differ from him, to the death,

[49] For a typical example, see "Poverty," *AYR*, XIII (24 June 1865),
512–15.
[50] "Plagues of London," *HW*, XI (5 May 1855), 316–19; "Gibbet
Street," *HW*, XIII (15 March 1865), 193–96.
[51] "Frost-Bitten Homes," *HW*, XI (31 March 1855), 193–96, and
"Pinchback's Cottage," *AYR*, VII (22 March 1862), 31–34; "Wild Court
Tamed," *HW*, XII (25 Aug. 1855), 85–87; "The Point of the Needle,"
AYR, X (5 Sept. 1863), 36–41; "The Belgian Lace-Makers," *HW*, I (29
June 1850), 320–23.
[52] Sir Edwin Chadwick, 1800–90, a sanitary reformer and protégé of
Jeremy Bentham. He became an investigator on the royal commission
on the poor laws in 1832, and with Nassau Senior drafted the Report of
1834 from which the New Poor Law grew. He broke with the actual
administration of the law because he favored a more centralized system of administration, and blamed the failures of the law on local mal-
administration. It was with Chadwick's belief in the efficacy of a
bureaucracy that Dickens differed.

on his crack topic — the New Poor-Law"; [53] and it is likely that he was suspicious of the law from the very beginning. Yet it is probable too that in the genesis of his political ideas Dickens was much indebted to the rational reformism of Bentham, and that not until roughly the date of *Hard Times* (1854) had he clarified even for himself the grounds of his differences with the Benthamites.[54] The Poor Law of 1834 applied the principles of political economy to the problem of the poor as stringently as common feeling and opinion could, under the circumstances, allow; and this Benthamite basis of the law may for a time have complicated Dickens' feelings against it. Certainly even when he conducted all-out war on the law, he concentrated his attack on the way it was administered, and in the postscript to *Our Mutual Friend*, he said of the law: "I believe there has been in England since the days of the STUARTS, no law so often infamously administered, no law so often openly violated, no law habitually so ill-supervised."

It is necessary to understand that the Poor Law of 1834 represented a break with the method of dealing with the poor that had been in operation since the time of Queen Elizabeth. Sidney and Beatrice Webb, in *English Poor Law Policy*,[55] give a useful account of the change produced by the Law of 1834; and even their prejudice on the subject, close in some ways to Dickens'

[53] *Letters* I, 480, to Austin, 25 September.
[54] See A. V. Dicey, *Lectures on the Relation between Law and Public Opinion in England during the Nineteenth Century* (London, 1905), pp. 418–22. Dickens' differences with the Manchester School are perhaps most explicit in a letter to Wills of 25 Nov. 1862 (*Letters* III, 321).
[55] (London, 1910), chs. i–iv.

own, helps to an understanding of Dickens' opposition. The Act of 1834 creates an administration but lays down no policy; it is the Report of 1834 that underlies the new policy. Central to the Report is the assertion made in the course of one argument, but never made as a recommendation, that the situation of the pauper should not be "really or apparently so eligible as the situation of the independent labourer. of the lowest class."[56] More plainly put, this asserts that pauperism must be made less desirable than the condition of people dependent for their subsistence on the most menial kind of work, or else it would soon be impossible to get people to do this menial work. In the course of the Report it is made clear that this applies to able-bodied laborers and their dependents, and not to orphans, or the aged, sick, or infirm.

If political economy had been strictly adhered to, the able-bodied would have had to work or starve, and the distinction between the pauper and "the independent labourer of the lowest class" would have been at its most persuasive. But popular sentiment would not have allowed this. The next best policy, then, was to keep the able-bodied pauper a scant distance from starvation, and thus make the undesirability of his situation clear. Of course there was another possibility — to improve the conditions of life of the menial laborer rather than lower the standards of the pauper. Dickens, or the Webbs, or humanitarians of many other descriptions would favor

[56] *Report from His Majesty's Commissioners for Inquiring into the Administration and Practical Operation of the Poor Laws* (London, 1834), p. 228. The theories of Malthus are clear behind this. See Elie Halévy, *The Liberal Awakening*, trans. E. I. Watkin, rev. ed. (London, 1949), pp. 40–41.

this alternative, but the Report of 1834 came out of the Benthamite climate.

The Report also recommended that responsibility for a policy in regard to paupers be taken from the individual parishes, to which it had been assigned during the reign of Elizabeth, and given to a central authority, which could then insure uniformity in the treatment of each class of destitute persons, reduce the shifting of paupers from one parish to another, prevent discontent among paupers, and bring the management more effectually under the control of Parliament. It recommended very strongly against the continuation of out-door relief (i.e., relief given outside a workhouse) for able-bodied laborers, because of the difficulty of discriminating according to merit in the award of such relief. It also set rules for "well-regulated workhouses."

But the principle of the Report of 1834 most heeded was that paupers not be treated too well. Treatment of paupers did not become as uniform as the writers of the Report had wished, varying a great deal from one workhouse to another; but the bad workhouses exceeded the good in number, and the total picture was certainly no encouragement to idle poverty. "Can any one wonder," Friedrich Engels asked, "that the poor decline to accept public relief under these conditions? That they starve rather than enter these bastilles?" [57] The examinations of poor-law practice frequently published in *Household Words* and *All the Year Round* reflect a similar point

[57] *The Condition of the Working-Class in England in 1844*, trans. F. K. Wischnewetzky, rev. Eng. ed. (London, 1892), p. 292. For conditions of workhouses, see Trevelyan, p. 250; or Elie Halévy, *The Triumph of Reform*, trans. E. I. Watkin, rev. ed. (London, 1950), pp. 284–85.

of view, and in one of these pieces an almost identical statement is made: "The principle upon which relief is administered under the law that taxes us for succour of the poor appears to be, to make the help rendered so distasteful, that they must be far gone indeed in wretchedness who will apply for it; and the high-hearted poor will starve rather than take it, will die instead of coming on the rates." [58] A few of these articles in the weekly periodicals merely describe the methods and problems of dealing with paupers, but most are directed against the Law of 1834, calling attention to such problems as overcrowding and actual lack of facilities in workhouses, particularly during hard winters, the inadequacy of medical help, the injustice of the residence requirements for relief, or the unfairness of having poor and rich parishes equally responsible for their own poor. [59]

What Dickens and other observers found reprehensible in the operation of the New Poor Law was the combination of inefficiency and a basic lack of charity. The word "charity" has often introduced confusion into discussions of Dickens' social views. Some specific things can be said about his view of charity, however, that will enlighten rather than confuse. Even the Benthamite framers of the New Poor Law did not think the law would obviate the further need for almsgiving. They wanted such charity to be private, not public, however, and depended on charity to provide what the law, in order to be consistent, could not provide: "Where cases of real hardship occur, the remedy must be applied by individual charity, a virtue

[58] "The Frozen-Out Poor Law," *AYR*, IV (16 February 1861), 446–49.

[59] For detailed reference to these articles, see Monroe Engel, "The Politics of Dickens' Novels," *PMLA*, LXXI (December 1956), 960–62.

for which no system of compulsory relief can be or
ought to be a substitute." [60] Dickens' insistence upon
charity, then, is far from singular. Where he breaks on
principle with the writers of the Report of 1834 is in
his belief that charity cannot be merely private but must
enter also into any government plan for dealing with
paupers, and in his belief in charity as a quality as well as
an activity. He insists that duty without love is not
enough.[61] He is scornful also of charity that is not disinterested, and an unpleasant story in *Household Words*
tells how a curate's use of alms to get the poor to attend
church finally demoralizes an entire community.[62]

Certain ideals of charity are indicated in the activities
of an order of begging nuns whose work is inferentially
compared to treatment of the poor by other agencies,
and in those of a man who is an exemplar of individually
conducted charity. Various charitable institutions are
also described and commented on, most notably the first
Children's Hospital in England. This hospital is reex-
amined ten years after its founding, and another hospital
in Liverpool, modelled on the first one in London, is also
described. Similar is the account of a visit to a foundling
hospital in London.[63] The need and justification for private charity is presented in "Houseless and Hungry,"

---

[60] *Report of 1834*, p. 263.

[61] Here the evidence of the fiction is valid and sufficient, but there
is also " 'I Have Done My Duty,' " *AYR*, XII (14 Jan. 1865), 543–46.

[62] "Our Parish Poor Box," IV (22 Nov. 1851), 204–07.

[63] "The Little Sisters," *HW*, IV (14 Feb. 1852), 493–94; "Little Blue
Mantle," V (24 July 1852), 429–31; "Drooping Buds," V (3 April 1852),
45–48 (this is the model for the children's hospital in *Our Mutual
Friend*); "Between the Cradle and the Grave," *AYR*, VI (1 Feb. 1862),
454–56; "One Other Hospital for Children," *HW*, XVIII (2 Oct. 1858),
379–80; "Received, A Blank Child," *HW*, VII (19 March 1853), 49–
53, ascribed to Dickens and Wills in Kitton.

in which the inmates of a shelter for the houseless-hungry are cast against the arguments of the extreme Malthusians and plain sceptics that there is no reason for such charity. A similar strategy lies behind two accounts of charity-financed homes for working girls whose earnings, even when they were employed, were not sufficient to enable them to live decently.[64]

But charity seemed to Dickens far more certainly a boon to the giver than to the receiver. He believed in self-help and independence and even perhaps in the salutary effect of work.[65] He was a hard as well as vulnerable man who had pulled himself up with the aid of a great talent, to be sure, but also by terrible determination and labor; and he expected other people to exert themselves, also. "You can no more help a people who do not help themselves, than you can help a man who does not help himself," he said. Similarly, he told two men who had asked him to join in a movement on behalf of working men that any such movement would be pointless until working people had begun to move on their own behalf.[66]

He liked to see men helping themselves, or men in a similar situation helping each other out of a sense of common interest. He gave publicity to examples of the poor banding together to help each other,[67] and he supported

[64] *HW*, XIII (23 Feb. 1856), 121–26; "Day-Workers at Home," *HW*, XIII (9 Feb. 1856), 77–78, and "Number Seven, Brown's-Lane," *AYR*, XII (5 Nov. 1864), 304–08.

[65] A rather maudlin story in *HW* tells how a working man rescues an army officer attempting suicide and rehabilitates him by giving him honest work to do. "Work! An Anecdote," I (6 April 1850), 35–36.

[66] *Letters* II, 652, to Layard, 10 April 1855; II, 774, to Ross and Kenny, 19 May 1856. See also the letter to Kenny written two days later.

[67] See, e.g., "Our Eye-Witness at a Friendly Lead," *AYR*, II (10 March 1860), 472–76.

any plan that would increase the economic independence
of the poor or laboring family. He favored the formation of provident societies, and he argued their superiority to parish charities. He published an article in favor
of post office savings banks; a recommendation of insurance as a joint social enterprise in which all take part
for mutual protection; an appeal for some kind of sick
insurance for railway clerks, who were early examples
of underpaid white-collar workers.[68]

In April of 1864, 1865, and 1866, *All the Year Round*
printed articles in favor of a government plan to sponsor
inexpensive insurance for workingmen, annuities for old
age and sickness.[69] Years before, an article in *Household
Words* had suggested that taxes should be a kind of insurance paid voluntarily by all members of the nation to
secure their rights and needs.[70] Together, all these articles suggest the possibility of a nation that does not so
much indulge in kindnesses toward those broken by life,
as try to recognize and insure the rights of its citizens
not to be so broken.

Dickens expected society to allow the workingman
his self-respect. It is notable that the comedy of the
working class characters in his novels does not often impinge on their dignity. When an article on workingmen's
clubs was being prepared for *All the Year Round*,

    [68] "Two Cures for a Pinch," *AYR*, VI (8 Feb. 1862), 462–67; "Parish
Charities," IX (23 May 1863), 308–09; "My Account with Her Majesty,"
XI (5 March 1864), 79–83; "Be Assured," *HW*, X (2 Dec. 1854), 365–69;
"Sick Railway Clerks," *HW*, XIII (19 April 1856), 325.
    [69] "Friendly or Unfriendly?" XI (9 April 1864), 202–04; "Poor
Men's Annuities," XIII (1 April 1865), 225–29; "A Post-Office Friendly
Society," XV (14 April 1866), 328–29.
    [70] "Taxes," XIV (6 September 1856), 181–85.

Dickens indicated the lines the article was to follow: that the men be trusted to manage their own affairs, including the problem of drunkenness among members, that they be neither babied nor patronized, and that social rest and recreation be made available to them as a needed respite without pretense of education.[71]

Money plays a big part in Dickens' novels, but it is also quite true that the ways in which people make money are not given concrete or detailed consideration. More can be learned about factories and industry in a novel by Mrs. Gaskell or even by Disraeli; more can be learned about financial transactions from Thackeray or George Eliot. Yet Dickens has a view of the place of finance and industry in the life of Victorian England that is always an operating force and sometimes a central operating force in his fiction. His attitude toward finance and speculation was simply hostile — he could see nothing good or real in it. Toward the growth of industry he had more mixed feelings, and tried to distinguish good from bad, and essential from incidental and aberrational.

Two articles in *Household Words* in 1855 and 1856 make certain terms of the attack on money very clear. The first derides the idea that social wrong can be made right by giving money to those wronged. The second is a plea for currency reform in which it is suggested that value is a function of labor and time.[72] In both arti-

[71] *Letters* III, 381, to Miss Manning, March 1864. The article appeared as "Working Men's Clubs," *AYR*, XI (26 March 1864), 149–54.

[72] "A Slight Depreciation of the Currency," XII (3 Nov. 1855), 313–15; "Moneysworth," XIII (31 May 1856), 461–64 (this seems closely related to Nassau Senior's view that value was a function of labor and abstinence).

cles, what is being opposed is the autonomous power of money.

The role of money and moneyed people in business is repeatedly attacked and ridiculed in the periodicals. An account of the activities of Petty, Larceny, and Co., for example, is a broad satire on financial ethics; and a description of the art of bankruptcy is written in much the same tone. Similar scorn is turned on rich directors of companies who have their positions only because they are rich, who know nothing about the businesses they are supposedly running, and who, when sitting on railway boards, for example, always vote against expenditures for safety devices. Again it is money as a license for departure from normal moral standards that is at the heart of Dickens' ire. Closely related is the objection to the practice of allowing officers in the army to buy their promotions.[73]

The sanctity that attends big business and the accumulation of money is particularly liable to attack by Dickens, in such accounts as that of the construction by a great hardware magnate of a hardware cathedral to the saint of hardware. The money transactions of the government are given little more dignity, and the whole structure of the national debt is made ludicrous by an examination of a representative group of the widows, cranks, old people, pensioners, and others to whom the debt is owed, who own thereby a share of the government. The hypocrisy and false front of money transac-

[73] "Twenty Shillings in the Pound," *HW*, XVI (7 Nov. 1857), 444–46; "Bankruptcy in Six Easy Lessons," *HW*, XVII (13 Feb. 1858), 210–12; "My Model Director," *HW*, XIX (26 Feb. 1859), 299–301; "Pay for Your Places," *AYR*, IV (27 Oct. 1860), 67–69. See also "Money or Merit?" *AYR*, III (21 April 1860), 30–32.

tions is illustrated by the story of a man who makes a living as a tout to a number of disreputable and socially unacceptable moneylenders while he himself keeps up the respectable appearance of a retired army officer.[74] The problem of debt, too, is brought into the general attack on money, by the observation that debt is a tragedy only for the little man; that for the big business man or financier, huge debts are a basis of power and esteem.[75] Again it is the capacity of money to reverse morality that Dickens hates.

For the most part the attack on money in *Household Words* and *All the Year Round* is not general or theoretical; it is launched specifically and in detail at the speculative "boom and bust" of the fifties and sixties. The expansion of British industry in these years and the opportunities for investment in the Empire and in other countries created a great need for capital, which the act of 1826 legalizing joint-stock banks outside the London area and the limited liability acts of 1855 and 1862 helped to provide.[76] Limited liability, which made "the liability of shareholders for the conduct of their company . . . purely pecuniary and limited to the amount of their investment," also made possible "the final step to stock-and-bond capitalism." Limited liability was granted to banking companies equally with other companies in 1858. Between 1856 (the year after the first limited liability act) and 1865 (the year before the panic of 1866)

---

[74] "A South Kensington Legend," *AYR*, VII (3 May 1862), 175–76; "Great Meeting of Creditors," I (11 June 1859), 153–56; "Accommodation," XIII (8 April 1865), 260–64.

[75] "Debt," *HW*, XVII (20 March 1858), 319–21.

[76] See C. R. Fay, *Great Britain from Adam Smith to the Present Day* (New York, 1928), pp. 110–13, 317.

the number of companies in Great Britain leaped from
227, with a nominal capital of 14 million pounds, to 1014,
with a nominal capital of 203 million pounds.[77]

This edifice collapsed in the panic of 1866. While it was
building, however, a vast new financial journalism was
created to publicize and support its needs and activities,[78]
so that *Household Words* and *All the Year Round* per-
formed a special function through their tendency to
consider this expansion as dangerous and unreal. The articles appeared with great frequency. One pictures a ghost
city populated by men ruined by speculation; two others
give an ironic history of a business boom stimulated by
the invention of a new improved patent corkscrew. The
Stock Exchange and the Paris Bourse are declared irra-
tional and immoral, and Dickens derides the idea that
they give the pulse of the country. That this is all part
of an attack on a false idolatry is made apparent by the
title and vocabulary of "The Golden Calf." "The City of
Unlimited Paper" is another warning of the fate of a
city that continues to worship these strange gods.[79]

More remarkable than the general terms of this cam-

[77] Leland Hamilton Jenks, *The Migration of British Capital to 1875*
(New York, 1927), pp. 234, 237–38. In 1864 there were fewer companies (975), but with a nominal capital of £235,000,000. In 1866, after
the panic, the number of companies dropped to 754, with a nominal
capital of £74,000,000. Two years later there were only 448 companies,
with a nominal capital of £33,000,000. In 1865 these companies issued
£122,000,000; in 1866, the year of the panic, they issued only £32,000,-
000.

[78] Jenks, pp. 254–55.

[79] "City Spectres," *HW*, IV (14 Feb. 1852), 481–85; "Provisionally
Registered," VII (9 July 1853), 445–48, and "Completely Registered,"
VIII (14 Jan. 1854), 469–71; "Bulls and Bears," *HW*, VIII (28 Jan.
1854), 517–23, and "On 'Change in Paris," *HW*, XIV (16 Aug. 1856),
102–08; "Phases of the Funds," *AYR*, V (6 July 1861), 342–46; *HW*, X
(23 Dec. 1854), 437–41; and XVII (19 Dec. 1857), 1–4.

paign against speculation is its specificity of detail. As
early as 1852, for example, there is a satiric account of
the failure of a joint-stock bank.[80] Though joint-stock
banks had a remarkable success during the expansion of
the fifties and sixties, Walter Bagehot in his classic account of the London money market, first published in
1873, still considered them a great potential danger.[81]
What disturbed Bagehot, and Dickens too, was the difficulty of exercising the control and supervision necessary
to keep the joint-stock banks honest and stable; and any
instability or failure could of course touch off a loss of
public confidence that in a credit economy creates panic
and disaster. *Crédit Mobilier*, a logical extreme of the
joint-stock bank, is treated as a magnificent example of
the need for greater government control.[82]

The satiric warnings against joint-stock companies and
certain related kinds of investment were very concentrated in *All the Year Round* in 1864 and 1865. This can
be attributed to more than chance or special personal preoccupation. Previously cited company figures show that
the boom reached a climax in 1864 and 1865 before
breaking in 1866. The Companies Act of 1862 and its
consequences induced many of the remaining private
banks — including in 1865 the greatest of the private
country banks, Lloyd's — to convert themselves into

[80] "The Great Chowsempoor Bank," *HW*, V (29 May), 237–40.
[81] *Lombard Street* (London, 1873). See the conclusion to the chapter entitled "The Joint Stock Banks."
[82] *HW*, XV (3 Jan. 1857), 8–12, and *AYR*, XX (27 June 1868), 57–
60. *Crédit Mobilier* was, as its name implies, a scheme to centralize
control and administration of a vast portion of a country's speculative
capital. The size and dangers of the scheme are apparent, and it would
likely be unmanageable even in a comparatively honest time, which this
was not. See Jenks, pp. 240–55.

joint-stock banks.[83] Construction too, including railway construction, was greater in the period 1860 to 1865 than ever before.[84]

The chicanery possible without stringent regulation is constantly pointed out, and evidently without much exaggeration of the facts of common occurrence. "Your Money and Your Life" relates how a bogus insurance company is set up, certain respectable innocents are persuaded to sit on its board of directors, policies are sold, but the company collapses when it cannot meet its first claim.[85] Stressed here, among other things, is one of the classic complaints against limited liability: that shareholders, even directing shareholders, do not have to take much responsibility for their companies.[86] The account of the Grand Financial and Credit Bank of Europe, Asia, Africa, America, and Australia (Limited) tells how this bank collapses when various firms in which it has invested fail, its depositors overdraw, and its stockholders panic and try to dump their stock.[87] Here again, something very close to the *Crédit Mobilier* idea is under fire.

"Going Into Business" is about the machinations of a Greek financier who sets up an international joint-stock company with branches in London, Smyrna, and Odessa.[88] The three firms or branches, with a total capi-

[83] Fay, p. 112.
[84] Jenks, p. 252.
[85] *AYR*, XI (30 April 1864), 275–80.
[86] For a summary of this line of argument from John Stuart Mill and others, see Jenks, pp. 235–36.
[87] "How We 'Floated' the Bank," *AYR*, XII (31 Dec. 1864), 493–97; "How the Bank Came to Grief," XIII (25 Feb. 1865), 102–06; "How the Bank was Wound Up," XIII (15 April 1865), 276–82.
[88] *AYR*, XIII (13 May 1865), 378–82; (20 May 1865), 404–08; (27 May 1865), 428–32.

tal of 300 pounds, draw upon each other in such a way that they create "a see-saw of bill-drawing, which often amounted to thirty or forty thousand pounds." This paper money is used to buy shares in other companies. Eventually, of course, the structure collapses. Everything in this account is carefully calculated to draw recognition from a contemporary reader. Even the choice of a Greek financier was not accidental, for Greeks were prominent in this period for their daring in the London money market.[89] One of these Greeks, Stefanos Xenos, wrote a book which casts some light on this process of creating capital: " 'To finance a company,' " he states, "is a technical phrase in use amongst the great City capitalists, and means nothing more than raising money after a certain fashion. Some person connected with the company that is to be 'financed,' draws bills, either from abroad or in England, upon said company; this paper is discounted by some bill-broker, and the money handed over to the company to meet urgent payments." [90]

Similarly topical is an account of attempts by a retired officer, who has sold his commission for 2600 pounds, to build that money into a fortune.[91] He is paid shares and money to give tone and respectability by his presence to the boards of directors of a bogus credit and finance company, The General House and Land Credit and Finance Company (Limited), and various largely bogus foreign investment companies which the finance company underwrites. What is reflected here is again the fi-

[89] Jenks, p. 246.
[90] *Depredations* (London, 1869), p. 47.
[91] "Amateur Finance," *AYR*, XIV (12 Aug. 1865), 56–60; (19 Aug. 1865), 87–91; (26 Aug. 1865), 110–15.

nance company conceived in terms of the *Crédit Mobilier* idea. This would have special meaning to a public aware that during early 1864, for example, the International Financial Society, Ltd. "floated a loan for the Danubian principalities . . . to build one railway, shares for the Lemberg-Czernowitz railway . . . , an Anglo-Italian Bank . . . , an Italian Land Company with a capital of a million and a half, a land company in Mauritius; and it cooperated with the *Crédit Mobilier* and Glyn, Mills, Currie in converting the entire Mexican debt. A reorganization of the Hudson's Bay Company, stock taken at 300 and issued to the public at 400, was of its most ambitious undertakings." [92]

Or again, "Starting the Rio Grande Railway" tells how two penniless adventurers turn railway promoters "on the 'limited liability' principle." [93] They put forward the idea that a railroad is needed from the Rio Grande to the City of Mexico, not because they know anything about it, but because "one spot seemed quite as good as another to set up a concern which was really never to have life, except what it derived from the printed prospectus." A bogus board of directors is set up; a joint-stock finance company is bribed to back the undertaking; and there is a fantastic rush to buy worthless stock. The shares having been sold, the market is artificially rigged

92 Jenks, p. 250.
93 *AYR*, XIV (11 Nov. 1865), 368–72; (18 Nov. 1865), 393–97. There had been a piece on an earlier era of railroad speculation also, "Ruined by Railways," *HW*, XI (3 March 1855), 114–19, about a man on his way to making a fortune in a railroad speculation until Parliamentary investigation brings on a crash, who is ruined and eventually throws himself under a train. The early piece is considerably less bitter, however, than the latter, perhaps because speculation did not then seem so utterly out of control.

to depress them, and they are then bought up low by a few insiders and boomed again — all this without reference to anything but a project. The pertinence of all this for a contemporary reader would have been great. Railways were being built more rapidly in this period even than in the forties,[94] and in 1864 and 1865 James Mc-Henry was bringing bond issues into the market with great success to support his fantastically unrealistic and unsuccessful Atlantic and Great Western Railway, into which he had never put a cent of his own money. No matter how badly his affairs went, people still rushed to invest their money.[95]

The general effect of the joint-stock company, and the effect likely to have been at the heart of Dickens' fears, was "to depersonalize business, to make of it a thing of by-laws not of men." [96] Dickens had no confidence ever in the healthy superseding of man's conscience by laws or things. He had similar fears about the depersonalization of industry. But to say he had this fear of industry — as he had of laissez-faire economic theory, or of centralized administration of paupers — is not to say that he failed to understand or engage with his own time, and that in his fear of the present and future he could only turn to the past.

Humphry House, in discussing the way Dickens mixes past and present, points out his constant use in his novels with contemporary themes of an earlier English scene of "inns and coaches, and gaiters and brass buttons." George Orwell makes the point that in "nearly all of his books one has a curious feeling that one is living in the first

[94] Jenks, p. 252.   [95] Jenks, pp. 255-59.
[96] Jenks, p. 233.

quarter of the nineteenth century." [97] What Orwell
might but does not go on to mention is that this immediate past serves the same function for Dickens that his
own immediate past does for Orwell himself, most markedly, say, in *Coming Up For Air*, in which the quarter
century between a man's boyhood and his early middle-
age represents the history of a progress from an orderly
gemütlich time when boys fished in secret pools and had
space around them, to a disordered, hurried, killing present. In such a use of the past, it is not the past itself that
is to be taken as hard fact and true, but what this imagined
past has to say about the real present. It is the creation of
an order, partly imaginary to be sure, against which disorder can be measured.

The point is that Dickens is not talking about the
superiority of the real past to the real present. He does
not reject industrial England in favor of pre-industrial
England. There are "hundreds of parrots," he says, "who
will declaim to you in speech and print, by the hour together, on the degeneracy of the times in which a railroad
is building across the water at Venice; instead of going
down on their knees, the drivellers, and thanking Heaven
that they live in a time when iron makes roads, instead
of prison bars and engines for driving screws into the
skulls of innocent men." Or again, he makes very much
the same point in regard to the way the telegraph "took
my fancy" — "piercing, like a sunbeam, right through
the cruel old heart of the Coliseum at Rome." Here there
is surely assent to the machines of the present. It is only
when Dickens fears that the machine is crowding out

[97] *The Dickens World* (Oxford, 1941), p. 18; "Charles Dickens,"
p. 50.

life that he is hostile to it; but this difference between the use and abuse of things is very nearly a constant in his view of society. It is significant too that the telegraph not only receives his assent, but also engages his "fancy," and in a letter to Forster he mentions an idea for a Christmas story about two groups of widely separated people joined "through the agency of an electric message." [98]

In a piece in *All the Year Round,* a mature man sums up the progress towards the millennium made in his lifetime. Most of the significant changes he discusses are the result of inventions — photography, the steam railway, gutta-percha, and so forth. Another article attacks the false romanticism of the Pre-Raphaelites and antiquarians who find a better life in the past than in the present, and contends that man's history is a history of progress — slow and difficult, but sure.[99] *Household Words* and *All the Year Round* publish factual descriptions of the growth and change of industrial cities like Lancashire and Liverpool, or call attention to the peculiarly vulnerable situation of the new unskilled laborer, and his need for education and security.[100] The problem of the displacement of men by machines is considered in two articles. The first of these does little more than recognize the fact that sewing machines are throwing seamstresses out of work, but the second, three years later, asserts that though machines may temporarily cause un-

[98] *Letters* I, 639, to Jerrold, 16 Nov. 1844; II, 533, to Mrs. Watson, 13 Jan. 1854; III, 302, 25 Aug. 1862.

[99] "Since This Old Cap Was New," II (19 Nov. 1859), 76–80; "The Bemoaned Past," VII (24 May 1862), 257–61.

[100] "Lancashire Witchcraft," *HW,* VIII (4 Feb. 1854), 549–51; "Our Sister," IX (1 July 1854), 471–74; "The Manchester Strike," XIII (2 Feb. 1856), 63–66.

employment, they will finally be not a threat to labor but a help, by improving the conditions of life and work.[101] Industrial accidents, too, are given attention. In the period 1854–55, the period previously noted as crucial for Dickens, the *Household Narrative* has many gruesome accounts of accidents in factories, and *Household Words* has frequent articles on this problem. Increasingly, the articles in *Household Words* are slanted at the failure of factory owners to take proper measures for the safety of their workers.[102] None of this bulks, of course, to a dominating interest in the problems of industrialization.[103] It adds, however, to the demonstration that Dickens had resolved the finance and industry of his time into his total sense of that time.

If a radical is one who goes to the root of things, then Dickens is a radical, and that preoccupation with the condition of man's heart that is sometimes held to be an indication of his political unreality is in fact the proof of his radicalism. But his radicalism was of an unorthodox sort. He was, first of all, anti-deterministic, and would not accept the idea that "nobody" was responsible for the ills of the world. He recognized no alternative to individual responsibility, not even in law, contending that

[101] "The Iron Seamstress," *HW*, VIII (11 Feb. 1854), 575–76; "Men Made by Machinery," XV (31 Jan. 1857), 97–100.

[102] Harriet Martineau wrote an attack on these articles which was published by the National Association of Manufacturers. *HW* replied with "Our Wicked Misstatements," XIII (19 Jan. 1856), 13–19. See also Johnson, pp. 854–55.

[103] Three other pieces should be made of record: "Children of All Work," *AYR*, V (8 June 1861), 254–58; and "Slavery in England," *AYR*, XVII (15 June 1867), 585–89 — both about child labor; also "The Rochdale Twenty-eight," *AYR*, XIX (29 Feb. 1868) 274–76 — an account of the beginnings of the English Cooperative Movement.

even justice cannot be merely left in the hands of the law, but must be each man's active concern.[104]

Then, too, until his hardening in 1854–55, at least, he was opposed to any extremism. This opposition continues even when his own analysis of the political and social situation is in most respects extreme. He believed that Cobbett had limited his usefulness to the cause of reform by being an extremist. He saw very readily the close connection between the extreme statement of a point of view and a burlesque of that point of view.[105]

The radical political movement of mid-nineteenth-century England, Chartism, had Dickens' nearly unmitigated contempt. In 1848, the year of the pyrrhic Chartist procession to Parliament, he wrote: "Chartist fears and rumours shake us, now and then, but I suspect the Government make the most of such things for their own purpose, and know better than anybody else how little vitality there is in them." The observation was peculiarly acute, for government agents were in fact actively trying to move the Chartists to their own ruin.[106] The following year he told Lady Burdett-Coutts "that while I feel for many working men who are chartists and mean no ill by it, I have no sympathy for the amateur members of that body"; and in 1851, a lead editorial in the *Household Narrative* attacked Chartism.[107] For many parts of

[104] "Nobody, Somebody, and Everybody," *HW*, XIV (30 Aug. 1856), 145–47; "Murderous Extremes," *HW*, XV (3 Jan. 1857), 1–2.

[105] See "Whole Hogs," *HW*, III (23 Aug. 1851), 505–07 — a general attack on extremism (ascribed to Dickens in Kitton); "Kensington Worthies," *HW*, VIII (3 Dec. 1853), 325–30; and "Vestiges of Protection," *HW*, XVII (2 Jan. 1858), 70–72, in which an extreme plea for free trade turns into a burlesque of the ideas it purports to support.

[106] *Letters* II, 103, to Moir, 17 June 1848; Elie Halévy, *Victorian Years*, trans. E. I. Watkin (London, 1951), p. 242.

[107] *Coutts Letters*, p. 150; *HN*, II (March–April 1851), 73.

the Chartist program, of course, he had sympathy, but for its extremism and its show of violence, particularly the theoretical violence of its gentlemen adherents, he had none. As we have seen, revolution seemed not a social instrument to him, but something to be dreaded.

Yet like most Victorians he was an activist, and believed it was necessary to do as well as know. To an oversensitive young lady who wrote to him for advice, he said: "The world is not a dream, but a reality, of which we are the chief part, and in which we must be up and doing something"; the "mystery" of the world, he went on, is not for us to brood over on earth. A few years later he wrote to another correspondent that "every day of my life I feel more and more that to be thoroughly in earnest is everything, and to be anything short of it is nothing." Increasingly, he expressed this earnestness by pointing out to the English on every possible occasion the "social evils and vices" which they did their best not to recognize,[108] and by undermining the false values and prides by which they lived and destroyed life. He was a subversive who undermined the accepted principles of his time, whether those principles related to representative government, class structure, the treatment of the poor, the making of money, or other subjects.[109] This special subversive instinct is clearly at work in all his fiction.

[108] *Letters* II, 203, to Miss Gotschalk, 1 Feb. 1850; II, 712, to Captain Morgan, circa Nov. 1855; II, 770, to Georgina Hogarth, 5 May 1856.
[109] Orwell calls Dickens subversive, but calls him also in the same sentence a radical and a rebel ("Charles Dickens," p. 2), which is to bury the real applicability of the one term with the limited applicability of the others. Wilson makes the important point when he says: "Of all the great Victorian writers, he was probably the most antagonistic to the Victorian Age itself" ("The Two Scrooges," p. 29).

PART TWO

Chapter Three

THE EARLY NOVELS

THE PICKWICK PAPERS

Dickens began writing *The Pickwick Papers* only eight days after the idea for some such book had first been proposed to him by the publisher William Hall. Actually, Hall had asked him to write sketches for a series of burlesque hunting scenes to be executed by the illustrator Seymour. This Dickens refused, but counter-proposed a substantially modified plan in which the illustrations would not dictate the text. The grounds of his objection to the Hall-Seymour proposal are worth noticing. Seymour's original idea was for a series of plates having to do with a Nimrod Club of cockney sportsmen — like those in Surtees' *Jorrocks' Jaunts and Jollities*, one of whose characters is in fact called Nimrod — whose adventures would turn into misadventures because they didn't really *know* how to ride or shoot, and were simply trying to imitate their social betters. Dickens objected that this was not a fresh idea, that the only country sport he knew much about was walking, and that his own imagination required and would willy-nilly pursue a freer range of scenes and people.[1] His objections on both commercial and personal grounds are symptomatic, in a novelist who made both a popular and an artistic success

[1] See Johnson, p. 117.

75

out of writing of his own interests and preoccupations.

But no matter how much Dickens was able to bend the initial plan of the book in the direction of his own interests, that he was able to start writing in only eight days not only shows his faith in his spontaneous resources, but also strongly suggests that he started without too much idea of where he was going. Two books, however, must to some extent have conditioned Dickens' expectations for this book on which he was embarking: his own *Sketches by Boz*, recently off the press, and Surtees' *Jorrocks*, which appeared first in 1831 — or at least the genre of which *Jorrocks* is the prime example. That there is a character in Surtees' book named Dickens is perhaps prophetic, but not much to the point. More substantial is the fact that Jorrocks himself and Pickwick have certain characteristics in common: both are heavy, carry telescopes, are fond of eating and drinking, are self-conscious dressers — though Jorrocks is far more flamboyant — and are leaders of a circle of men mostly younger than themselves. There is something similar, too, in Pickwick's woman-eschewing bachelorhood and Jorrocks' marriage to a harridan whose existence he does his best to overlook. And Jorrocks' scrape with the law, for trespassing, is narrated with something of the tone that Dickens later employs in developing the case of Bardell vs. Pickwick, though the incident itself is more suggestive of the one that brings Pickwick to the pound. The attitude toward legal process and the legal profession is similar in both writers: as when Surtees talks of "Mr. Smith, a goodish-looking man for a lawyer"; or in the mixture of false eloquence and crude invective with which the sergeants-at-law conduct their cases; or, and most particularly, in the manifestly unfair judgments that conclude both cases.

Beyond all this, there is a slight but repeated suggestion of Quixote in Surtees' treatment of Jorrocks that is augmented in Dickens' treatment of Pickwick, and underlies the kind of dignity with which Pickwick eventually emerges. When Jorrocks is trying to find his way on horseback in a fog, Surtees talks of his "Quixotic undertaking," and a few pages later a groom recommends a horse to Jorrocks as willing to leap anything, even "a windmill with the sails going." The suggestion is there, but not strongly, and with little consistency and almost no depth, for Jorrocks rarely suggests more than the hallucinated buffoon element of Quixote's character. Nor had Dickens need of Surtees to remind him of *Quixote*, which had been one of the influential and much-read books of his childhood.

Toward the schematic side of *Jorrocks* — the comic hunting scenes — Dickens makes only a few passing gestures: Mr. Winkle's lack of proficiency with a gun or a horse, for example, or Mr. Tupman's accidental and amazed shooting of a bird. Even giving every chance similarity its greatest weight, it is hard to find *Pickwick* very significantly indebted to *Jorrocks* — and most of such debt as there is or may be (the Quixote overtone aside) does not much involve the real achievement of *Pickwick*.

The *Sketches by Boz*, however, throw great light on Dickens' later development. As important as anything is the distinctive sense of London, Dickens' most intensely realized place throughout his work. Any one of the titles of the section of the *Sketches* called "Scenes"

will suggest a cluster of scenes and actions from *The
Pickwick Papers* and the succeeding Dickens novels of
the next quarter-century. But it is not just place as physical or visual setting that is suggested by these sketches.
The approach to place is already a matter of tone, style,
or — more generally — point of view. For Dickens is the
true city-dweller who sees the city as the miniature of
the world, and who in addition is drawn not so much to
its civilized surface as to the seething suffering below.
It is the great sea of human misery — to put it in Dickensian terms — that holds his imagination, and this is
most available to that imagination as it presents itself in
the city.

This may not seem immediately pertinent to *The Pickwick Papers*, whatever its pertinence to the later novels.
Yet any more careful consideration cannot fail to reveal
that underlying this book's gaiety — and quite often
breaking through it — is a deep melancholy.[2] Immediately pertinent, too, is the keen delineation in the
Sketches of the striving pretensions of the insecure lower
middle class; and the brutalization of those just beneath
them; and the callousness of those above.

But if Dickens has much of his scene already in the
Sketches, he has it more by experience and first instinct
than by force of mind. Nor does he yet have the literary
force to make much of it. This is shown, as well as anywhere, by the death at the end of the sketch called
"The Drunkard's Death," in which a man whose drinking causes the degradation and ruin of his family finally
— overcome by the sense of what he has done — decides
to kill himself. The writing here is not ineffectual, but it

2 Wilson has, of course, shown this most dramatically.

has little of that extensive power of generalization that will later make similar scenes in Dickens almost unbearable. Advance in this regard can be seen already in *The Pickwick Papers*: as, for example, in the death of the Chancery prisoner in the Fleet, in which the reader is implicated to a far greater extent than he can be in the death of the drunkard. This, even though Dickens sees them both — though of course to varying degrees — as social victims. Part of the difference has to do with timing or pace; as Dickens becomes more sure of what is peculiarly his own subject matter, he allows himself to hover, to linger more, and to let these subjects amass their obsessive power.

But the increase in strength from the *Sketches* to *The Pickwick Papers* is little more startling than the progress as a writer of fiction that Dickens makes within *The Pickwick Papers*. The book commences as something close to another collection of sketches — better sketches, but still sketches — and ends as something close to a novel. The most apparent change is probably that caused by the introduction of underlying, complicating, and continuing situations to bind together the succession of events. The chief plot element in *The Pickwick Papers* is the case of Bardell vs. Pickwick, which grows from an incident in Chapter XII, but does not really become a case, and a continuing narrative complication, until Chapter XVIII. Other extended complications of this order, but lesser, are provided by the pursuit of Alfred Jingle and Job Trotter; the running feud between Weller, Sr., and his wife over the red-nosed temperance preacher Stiggins; and the romantic activities of Pickwick's young friends Winkle and Snodgrass. All these plot elements are, in one way or another, romantic, and all involve, in one way or another, problems of disguise or false appearance.

But beyond these rather meagre gestures toward plot — beyond them in importance for the coherence and power of this novel — is the really fundamental movement of the book in the direction of gravity, seriousness, profundity. One instance of this, a miniature of the general progress of the novel, is the changing nature of the case of Bardell vs. Pickwick itself. In its beginnings nothing could be more ludicrous than this misunderstanding and its consequences, with the plump virtuous Pickwick requesting his amorous widowed landlady to send her son away, and then asking her: "Mrs. Bardell . . . Do you think it a much greater expense to keep two people, than to keep one?"

It is a certain, a predictable formula, really a burlesque scene, ending with Mrs. Bardell fainting in the arms of the astonished and confused Pickwick just as his friends Tupman, Winkle, and Snodgrass arrive to visit him. Of course he protests his innocence, and of course they take the situation slyly, concur in all his excuses, but do not believe him. The situation is complete, and there is no way to determine whether at this point Dickens had any intention of making any further use of a conventional comic incident. Considerably later, but with no intervening mention of what has happened, Pickwick receives a letter from a couple of sharp-practicing attorneys, Dodson and Fogg, informing him that they have been retained by Mrs. Bardell "to commence an action against you for a breach of promise of marriage." The original comic cast of the incident is recalled by the reaction of

Wardle, who calls Pickwick a "sly dog" and laughs so hard that the glassware on the sideboard rings.

But the intelligence that underlies Pickwick's consternation now gives the incident additional dimension. He says:

"It's a conspiracy . . . a base conspiracy between these two grasping attorneys, Dodson and Fogg. Mrs. Bardell would never do it; — she hasn't the heart to do it; — she hasn't the case to do it. Ridiculous — ridiculous . . . It's a vile attempt to extort money."

This combination of acumen and accurate generosity under stress is impressive. But his faith in justice is unfounded, and Dodson and Fogg get a judgment against him even though Sam Weller reveals in court that they have taken the case on speculation. When his sense of justice will not let him agree to this judgment, and he goes to prison rather than pay up and, by so doing, concur in injustice, Pickwick comes his closest to Quixotic stature: a preposterous and noble victim of his own principles, suffering but adamant, opposing injustice and aiding the downtrodden, forgiving even those who have wronged him, and attended by his worldly, sceptical, but devoted Sancho, Sam Weller.

The scenes in the Fleet provide a considerable prevision of the Dickens to come — of the mind and sensibility made incandescent by poverty, injustice, suffering, and social oppression. For considerable stretches here, Dickens forgets that he is supposed to be writing comedy. We have, to be sure, Pickwick springing to the defense of his nightcap, and Stiggins lecturing Sam Weller on contrition, but for the most part this section of the novel is no more comic than the prison scenes in *David Copperfield* or *Little Dorrit*. Overt seriousness falls off again, after the Fleet, and after Pickwick has had to concede to Dodson and Fogg in order to spare Mrs. Bardell, which is in itself a serious comment on the limitations of justice. But the remainder of the novel, though less overtly serious, is acted out under the shadow of the Fleet, as it were — it is a bringing together and finishing, so that Pickwick can lapse into a retired, benevolent old age.

To examine the development of Pickwick from ridiculousness to dignity is one way to get at the growing seriousness of the novel, and at the rise of Dickens' fuller powers within the novel. Another way of getting at what is latent in *The Pickwick Papers* — and sometimes overt — is to look at the first several of the interpolated stories that are a regular feature of Volume I, and are scattered, only less frequently, through Volume II: [3]

I. The story variously called "The Stroller's Tale" or, pointedly, "Dismal Jemmy's Tale": an account of the death of a pantomine actor, an habitual drunkard, who transforms his guilty feelings toward his wife, whom he has neglected and abused, into a fear that she is going to murder him for revenge.

II. "The Convict's Return": a narrative about a cruel, dissolute man who abuses his wife and drives his son to crime; the son is transported, and the wife dies of grief; when the son finally returns, and confronts his father, the old man attacks him but dies of a stroke.

III. "A Madman's Manuscript": a similarly morbid story of a madman who conceals his madness, amasses

[3] Wilson, again, has illuminated the significance of these stories.

a fortune, uses his money to marry a girl who loves someone else, purposely torments and finally kills her, and
then runs openly mad and ends his life in an asylum.

IV. "The Bagman's Story": a lighter and jollier story,
of Tom Smart, who marries a handsome widow who
owns an inn; but Tom's triumph is made possible by the
good offices of a grotesquely carved chair that comes to
life and gives him information and good advice. Though
cheerful, the story is decidedly macabre.

V. "The Parish Clerk": a tale in which an ugly ridiculous parish clerk is used as a foil by a pretty neighbor-
ing girl who pretends to be in love with him in order to
camouflage the real romance she is carrying on — breaking the heart, such as it is, of the clerk when he discovers
the truth.

There are many more interpolated stories, and they
go on in much the same morbid, depressing, pathetic,
and even bathetic way, contributing heavily to the ac-
cretive weight of seriousness of this novel that seems to
begin so largely as farce.

The place of personal loyalties contributes to this seriousness also: the loyalty of Pickwick and his friends,
even of Job Trotter to Alfred Jingle, and most conspic-
uously of Sam Weller to Pickwick. Sam's place as Sancho Panza to Pickwick's Quixote gives schematic justification to the practical nature of his intelligence, and to
the peculiar aphoristic mannerisms that stud his speech.
His is the voice of worldly wisdom, of shrewdness, of
that knowledge Dickens thinks of as derived out-of-
doors and from experience — survival knowledge. He
has the education that tells him where he will and where
he won't get a shilling. Tony Weller says of his son:

"I took a good deal o' pains with his eddication, sir; let him run in the streets when he was very young, and shift for his-self. It's the only way to make a boy sharp, sir." What distinguishes Sam Weller, however, is that his heart survives even this education.

"No, no; reg'lar rotation, as Jack Ketch said, wen he tied the men up!" This construction is the identifying mark of Sam's language — and to a lesser extent of his father's, from whom he learned it. His "as" clause is a special kind of aphorism, only superficially apposite, bringing together but not much reconciling largely distant matters, and thus engendering the comedy of discrepancy or incongruity, while at the same time, in the guise of common wisdom, making a joke of the very possibility of wisdom:

"That's the pint, sir, out vith it, as the father said to the child, wen he swallowed a farden."

"There's nothin' so refreshin' as sleep, sir, as the servant-girl said afore she drank the egg-cupful o' laudanum."

"I think he's the wictim o' connubiality, as Blue Beard's domestic chaplain said, with a tear of pity, ven he buried him."

"He's a ma-licious, bad-disposed, vorldly-minded, spiteful, windictive creetur, with a hard heart as there ain't no soft'nin'. As the wirtuous clergyman remarked of the old gen'l'm'n with the dropsy, ven he said, that upon the whole he thought he'd rayther leave his property to his vife than build a chapel vith it."

"Hows'ever, it was to be — and wos, as the old lady said arter she'd married the footman."

Language — and particularly spoken language — is the major distinction *The Pickwick Papers* has over its predecessors: over those books like *Jorrocks*, which are to some extent its predecessors in a genre; and over Dickens' own previous fiction, the *Sketches by Boz.* Besides the two Wellers, father and son, there is the weeper, Job Trotter, and Alfred Jingle too. A reviewer reading *Pickwick* as the work of an unknown novelist, might well have found in the introduction of Jingle, with his peculiar shorthand-of-the-mind speech, a mark of possible genius:

"Heads, heads — take care of your heads!" cried the loquacious stranger, as they came out under the low archway, which in those days formed the entrance to the coach-yard. "Terrible place — dangerous work — other day — five children — mother — tall lady, eating sandwiches — forgot the arch — crash — knock — children look around — mother's head off — sandwich in her hand — no mouth to put it in — head of a family off — shocking, shocking! Looking at Whitehall, sir? — fine place — little window — somebody else's head off there, eh, sir? — he didn't keep a sharp look-out enough either — eh, sir, eh?"

Perhaps this is the cue to proportion. For primarily *The Pickwick Papers* is a comedy of extraordinary energy, range, and compassion, most memorable for its intensely comic moments: Mr. Winkle's horse moving sideways; Pickwick in a strange lady's bedchamber; Tupman proposing to Miss Wardle; and the brilliantly original comic voices of Tony and Sam Weller, and of Alfred Jingle.

Oliver Twist

In the corpus of Dickens' novels, there is none — with the possible exception of *Hard Times* — more purposeful than *Oliver Twist,* which starts with a birth in a work house and ends (excepting the conventional last summary chapter) with the hanging of Fagin. These are the general subjects between which the story moves: poverty and crime, and the connections between them. In its purposeful coherance, *Oliver Twist* is at a far remove from *The Pickwick Papers*. Since it was begun, however, when Dickens was little more than half finished with *Pickwick*, the contrast is peculiarly interesting. But to make sense of the contrast, allowance must be made first for the imposed differences.

The Pickwick Papers was written for publication in twenty individual monthly parts. This was to become Dickens' favorite and most frequently used form of publication. *Oliver Twist*, however, was to appear serially in *Bentley's Magazine* (a monthly), in relatively short installments, surrounded of course by other fiction and articles. It was to be roughly half the length of *The Pickwick Papers*, and to be published in shortish stretches, and would require special coherence to distinguish it from the other material with which it appeared.

In addition to noting these facts of difference, it is tempting to make certain speculations. Writing two novels simultaneously and at great speed, Dickens might well have required gross difference to keep his own mind and imagination clear. Moreover, he commenced *Oliver Twist* at more or less the time that he was discovering the function of plot in *The Pickwick Papers*, and he may have wished for the chance to make some fuller exploitation of plot, to write a novel whose parts were consequent as well as sequent.

But the form of this shorter novel designed for magazine publication seemed to Dickens himself to impose certain limitations and difficulties. *Hard Times*, *Great Expectations*, and *A Tale of Two Cities* are written in roughly the same form, and have certain characteristics in common with *Oliver Twist*, but for them the difficulties were even greater because the parts appeared weekly rather than monthly. The 20 part novel Dickens associated with "the large canvas and the big brushes,"[4] and he complained once to Forster of the "crushing" difficulty of the shorter-type novel for a writer who had "had an experience of patient fiction-writing with some elbow-room always, and open places in perspective."[5]

But how, specifically, does this difference evidence itself to the reader? In an edition of Dickens in which *The Pickwick Papers* is 968 pages long, *Oliver Twist* is 510 pages long — roughly 2:1. *Pickwick* is divided into 57 chapters averaging 17 pages each. *Oliver Twist* has 53 chapters — only four less — but they average a little under 10 pages each. Since the chapter is, by and large, a genuine unit for Dickens, the difference between a chapter of 17 pages and a chapter of 10 pages suggests a radically different pace of narration.

For example, *The Pickwick Papers* begins with "the perusal of the following entry in the Transactions of the Pickwick Club, which the editor of these papers feels the highest pleasure in laying before his readers, as a proof of the careful attention, indefatigable assiduity, and nice discrimination, with which his search among the multifarious documents confided to him has been conducted." There follows a pompous, windy, circumlocu-

---

[4] *Letters* III, 378, to Collins, 24 January 1864.
[5] *Letters* II, 543, February 1854.

tory account of the resolution to form The Correspond-
ing Society of the Pickwick Club; a florid description
of Pickwick himself; an account in indirect discourse
of a speech by Pickwick; also of a petty altercation between
Pickwick and Mr. Blatton of Aldgate. Everything about
this suggests leisure, not least of all the indirect discourse
in which a good part of it is cast. The personal qualities
that the "editor of these papers" boasts of or lays claim to
also promise leisure: the "careful attention, indefatigable
assiduity, and nice discrimination" brought to bear on these
"multifarious documents."

The chapter of roughly four pages that begins *Oliver
Twist* is in marked contrast. Oliver's birth in a workhouse is recorded in the first paragraph. The briskness
of the narrative is not so much seen or felt as insisted
on when Dickens tells us, for example, that it will be
prudent to omit the real name of the town in which the
workhouse is located and that he will not bother to assign
it a fictitious name, any more than he will bother to give
the day and date of the event, since they do not matter; or
that he will not take time to repeat Oliver's name, referring to him instead, to save time, as "the item of mortality whose name is prefixed to the head of this chapter."
In this first paragraph, more space is spent in talk about
saving space than in anything else. Yet, funny as this
may be, it does tend to prepare the reader for the genuine speed with which things are to happen. Oliver's
mother dies on page 3, and on page 4 we get a suggestion
of her general history as an unwed mother. In these four
pages, too, we are given an attitude toward the workhouse and public care of paupers, and a considerable
amount of specific detail about these facilities. Three

pages farther on, Oliver is nine years old. The novel
moves swiftly throughout, though not at this pace, of
course, or it would be close to the ideal of brevity Dickens suggests on page one — a novel about a hero who
dies at birth.

The plot of *Oliver Twist*, too, is conceived and han-
dled economically, proceeding pretty much on the single
strand of Oliver's adventures and misadventures, with no
elaborately divergent sub-plots, and not much more attention to the lives and idiosyncrasies of the other characters than is necessary to bring them into Oliver's story
with force. The purposefulness of *Oliver Twist* gives it
its power, its unrelenting grasp on what Dickens would
have called its "truth," the connection between misery
and the criminal life. Oliver Twist begins his life in
misery enough — orphaned, underfed, unloved, beaten,
apprenticed in time to an undertaking establishment
where he is bullied, fed the scraps the dog scorns, and
made to sleep in the shop with the coffins at night. Finally,
when his mother's memory is insulted, he rebels and runs
away to London, carrying with him his total means: the
torn clothes on his back, an extra shirt, two pairs of
darned stockings, a crust of bread, and a penny. When
he reaches the outskirts of London, he is seen by the
Artful Dodger, who, being a considerable social philosopher, knows that his starving bedraggled condition
makes him a likely candidate for Fagin's gang of pickpockets and thieves. For it is the criminals themselves
who — generally without sentimentality, simply as recognition of the way things work — know best the roots
and causes of crime. Even Bill Sikes, who is not notably
intellectual, knows them in his own way:

"I want a boy, and he musn't be a big un. Lord! . . . if I'd
only got that young boy of Ned, the chimbley-sweeper's! He
kept him small on purpose, and let him out by the job. But
the father gets lagged; and then the Juvenile Delinquent Society comes, and takes the boy away from a trade where he was
arning money, teaches him to read and write, and in time
makes a 'prentice out of him. And so they go on, . . . so
they go on; and, if they'd got money enough (which it's a
Providence they haven't), we shouldn't have half-a-dozen
boys left in the whole trade, in a year or two."

Misery is not a matter of conjecture for Dickens, but
a terrible presence. It means, for example, the "bleak,
dark, and piercing cold," when "the homeless, starving
wretch" has little to do but "lay him down and die.
Many hunger-worn outcasts close their eyes in our bare
streets, at such times, who, let their crimes have been what
they may, can hardly open them in a more bitter world."
Following Oliver on the job with the undertaker Sowerby,
the reader gets a vivid picture of what Dickens means by
misery — the dreadful deprivation of food, shelter, medical
care, creature comfort, the deprivation in fact of all the
social mitigations that man can muster against the awful,
immitigable fact of mortality. Sometimes Dickens' sense
of the real situation falters or grows dim in its details
and applications, and produces bathos, as when Oliver
says farewell to the orphan Dick, or when Dick's dying
request is to give his "dear love to poor Oliver Twist."
These moments are comparatively few, though, and do
not much damage the genuine vision of a misery sufficiently desperate to make a boy wish for the calm sleep
of death, or to drive him into depravity.

But it is clear that Dickens does not mean that the de-

praved are not responsible for their depravity, that they
are simply victims of their misery. Oliver, after all,
despite his misery and the pressures brought upon him
by Fagin and his gang, retains his innocence and even
does no wrong, whereas Monks does evil not because he
has been forced to evil, but because he is a corrupt man.
Dickens believes that there is innate evil and innate goodness, and that true innocence is in some way its own
defense. Not even Fagin is unsusceptible to Oliver's innocence, and it is significant for the moral strategy of
the novel that Monks and Oliver are half-brothers.

In his Preface to *Oliver Twist,* Dickens says part of his
purpose was to paint a picture of criminal life so realistically unattractive that it would throw no false romance
about crime, and might even serve as a deterrent to the
life of crime:

It appeared to me that to draw a knot of such associates in
crime as really did exist; to paint them in all their deformity,
in all their wretchedness, in all the squalid misery of their
lives; to show them as they really were, for ever skulking
uneasily through the dirtiest paths of life, with the great
black ghostly gallows closing up their prospect, turn them
where they might; it appeared to me that to do this, would
be to attempt a something which was needed, and which would
be a service to society. And I did it as I best could.

This statement was made primarily as a defense against
the charge that the book's realism was offensive, and as
such no modern reader will quarrel with it. The modern
complaint is more likely to be that Dickens is not realistic
enough. But in any broader context, is this protest of intentions quite convincing? Isn't Dickens, as Edmund

Wilson has so illuminatingly argued, fascinated as well
as revolted by depravity? The answer to the question at
its crudest is quite clear: there is no simple, exclusive
revulsion in Dickens' view of criminals. Nor is there
much doubt that to some extent at least this ambiguous
point of view is pre-rational or subconscious. But Dickens is a far more rational, controlled writer than is generally allowed, and the ambiguous view and role of the
criminal in *Oliver Twist* is in good part rational and intended, and is related to and serves his general view of
his society.

The view of institutional society in *Oliver Twist* is
clear enough — the view of the police and courts, the
workhouse and parish administration, the House of
Commons in which Harry Maylie must give up his ambitions in order to marry Rose Fleming. Institutional
society is immoral, inefficient, stupid, unfeeling, and —
perhaps worst of all, aesthetically — unheroic. Wher-
ever institutions touch, people are corrupted, acquiring
a corporate, collective, or administrative view of life,
rather than an individual humane view.

The criminal in *Oliver Twist* is not simply the enemy
of institutional society — of the police, the courts, the
lawmakers. He is also in some degree heroic and guided
by a peculiar, limited moral code. He is part too of a
society whose common members at least are quick, spontaneous, fun-loving, and convivial. To get the significance of this last consideration, compare the mean cheer-
lessness of the workhouse, or the undertaker's shop, with
the first view of the thieves' den, with its easy-going,
fraternal shelter, and Fagin himself preparing a generous
meal of sausage for everybody, of which Oliver is at

once invited to partake. The horseplay is rough but largely good-humored. Even Fagin's school for pickpockets is conducted like a stylized game, and his constant and sinister use of the phrase "my dear" has a color of affection to it, perverted though it be, completely lacking from the cold ministrations of Bumble or Mrs. Mann.

The courage of the thieves is at its least a brilliant bravado. This is most immediately apparent in the language of the Artful Dodger, John Dawkins, another one of those brilliant eccentric languages that Dickens creates, reminiscent in originality and energy of the language of the Wellers and Alfred Jingle. His bravado before the court, for example, is moving because it is in the face of heavy consequences. The point is not only that the criminals are threatened by death, but that they are all of them, even the most hardened, aware of the imminence of this threat almost all the time. When Sikes and Nancy have abducted Oliver and are hurrying him to Fagin's, they hear the bell sounding from the jail:

"Eight o'clock, Bill," said Nancy, when the bell ceased.

"What's the good of telling me that; I can hear it, can't I?" replied Sikes.

"I wonder whether *they* can hear it," said Nancy.

"Of course they can," replied Sikes. "It was Bartlemy time when I was shopped; and there warn't a penny trumpet in the fair, as I couldn't hear the squeaking on. Arter I was locked up for the night, the row and din outside made the thundering old jail so silent, that I could almost have beat my brains out against the iron plates of the door."

"Poor fellows!" said Nancy, who still had her face turned towards the quarter in which the bell had sounded. "Oh, Bill, such fine young chaps as them!"

"Yes; that's all you women think of," answered Sikes. "Fine young chaps! Well, they're as good as dead, so it don't much matter."

Bravado with this consciousness becomes something more profound.

In the Preface, Dickens says too that he does not want to make the thieves' world seem glamorous as it does in Gay's *Beggar's Opera,* and the romantic glamor that Gay employs with Macheath and Polly is certainly absent from *Oliver Twist* — is, specifically, no part of the relationship of Nancy and Sikes. But it is a related world nonetheless that Dickens pictures, where the thieves, in danger from the law and from the leaders in their own hierarchy both, are part of a rapacious society in which every man is alone and there is neither order nor kindness. For Dickens' interest in the thieves' world is at least as much political as neurotic, part of the subversive view of English society that he seems to have held always, and held with increasing strength and consciousness as he grew older. *Oliver Twist* is a novel about society, as all of Dickens' novels that follow are too, and as even *The Pickwick Papers* became before it was finished. We move out from the child in the workhouse in a nameless town to the world at large, and to a picture of the terror of life against which society offers not even the few comforts it could. At the end of *Oliver Twist,* Dickens effects one of those savings of character from type that are his tribute to the complexity of life. For even Fagin, in his cell, is human, mortal, alone, and afraid.

NICHOLAS NICKLEBY, THE OLD CURIOSITY SHOP,
BARNABY RUDGE, MARTIN CHUZZLEWIT

Between *Oliver Twist* and *Dombey and Son,* Dickens,
working quickly and voluminously, failed to produce
a novel that is — from the vantage of modern taste, which
sets a higher value on coherence or unity in fiction than
did the eighteenth or, until near the end, the nineteenth
century — a sustained success. Dickens started writing
Nicholas Nickleby in February of 1838, while he was
still working on *Oliver Twist,* and finished it in September of 1839. It was written in twenty monthly parts, like
The Pickwick Papers. The Old Curiosity Shop was commenced early in 1840 and finished in January of 1841.
It was written in weekly installments, at first worked into
a frame story called *Master Humphrey's Clock,* though
this frame was soon dropped. *Barnaby Rudge,* also first
conceived for *Master Humphrey's Clock,* began appearing
in February 1841, a month after Dickens had finished
writing *The Old Curiosity Shop,* but some of it had been
written earlier. *Barnaby Rudge* was finished in November of 1841. *Martin Chuzzlewit* was begun in late 1842
and finished in the middle of 1844. It was written in
twenty monthly parts, the form of *The Pickwick Papers*
and *Nicholas Nickleby* and that in which Dickens was
to do most of his major fiction. Between February 1838
and the middle of 1844, then, Dickens wrote the end of
Oliver Twist, four other long novels, *American Notes,*
and a number of shorter items of fiction and non-fiction.
He was writing under great pressure, but in a spirit
nevertheless of experimentation and way-seeking. These

four novels have much in common: they are all, to varying extents, novels of the road; all have marked exploitation of what Dickens himself, in his Preface to *The Old
Curiosity Shop*, called the "grotesque and wild, but
not impossible"; all have a hard core of social seriousness.
They have, too, strong thematic similarities.

No writer of great stature has kept more persistently
to his own themes than did Dickens. They inform his
writing from first to last, welling from the great, brood-
ing, obsessive center of his mind's most fertile life to in-
spirit his work with its most intense energies. In the
thirty-five years or so of his career as a writer of fiction,
Dickens almost never repeats himself. His inventive
power is enormous, and the range of his knowledge and
interests wide. But behind all that he writes is a point of
view that develops, to be sure, but does not change essentially. In part this point of view is merely a matter of
opinions and prejudices. But opinion is not likely to be
the most interesting part of an artist's mind. A more interesting aspect of point of view — more interesting because more revealing and more related to what gives art
power — are those recurrent configurations of experience to which an artist's imagination responds. In Dickens' fiction, a unique and powerful efflorescence is ex-
cited by certain themes which occupy a central or symbolically critical place in his view of his world. The
naming of a theme, because it is not so much a fixed
category as an individual and often eccentric creation of
the mind, is not easy. But some of the themes of these
four novels can be roughly indicated as money and its
disfigurements; poverty, and the insufficiency of gov-

ernment and institutions to deal with it; individual benevolence; unseemly marriages; criminality; the death of the young and innocent.

Nicholas Nickleby was begun before Dickens had finished *Oliver Twist*; and as the subject of *Oliver Twist*, in a sense, is the deficiencies of the poor-law system, so that of *Nicholas Nickleby* is the "ragged schools" of Yorkshire — cheap, brutal boarding schools in which the students were neither educated, nurtured, nor even adequately housed and clothed. Yet *Nicholas Nickleby* is no more a "problem novel" than was its predecessor. Dickens' sense of the life about him was too teeming, vivid, and detailed, to be shaped into such confines, and the "ragged schools," as a problem and subject, were less immediately and diversely linked to Dickens' dominating interests than was poor-law administration.

Much of the vitality of *Nicholas Nickleby*, then, as a novel, is elsewhere, and much of it is related to the themes enumerated. To money and its disfigurements, first of all. Nicholas Nickleby's father dies of a broken heart when — chafed by the smallness of his fortune, and foolishly encouraged by his wife — he speculates with what money he has and loses everything. His elder brother Ralph is a usurer by profession and extremely rich, but pretends to have little or nothing, and leads a miserable, miserly life, goaded always by his yen for gold and his malevolent feelings. Arthur Gride is a shrinking version of the same usurious breed, who conspires to marry a beautiful young girl, Madeline Bray, not out of lechery but out of avarice, having found papers that prove her heir to a great fortune. Madeline's father is disfigured in a different way by money. He lusts for it nearly as much as do Ralph Nickleby and Gride, but he wishes to squander, not harbor it.

Against the machinations for money, neither government nor institutions bring any sufficient force for good. The unprotected — Smike, for example, the kidnapped and abandoned son of Ralph Nickleby — are ground down by poverty and its attendant, poor health; and education, which should teach justice, is instead hand-in-glove with injustice. The failure of recourse in government or institutions is made up for in part by personal benevolence. The benevolence of Nicholas is Smike's one protection, and he in turn is saved by the benevolence of the Cheeryble brothers, good–natured and astonishingly clean-handed tycoons. The fact that Dickens based the Cheeryble brothers on two actual tycoons, the brothers Daniel and William Grant of Ramsbottom and Manchester, does not answer the objections to them. We feel, with justice, that something is missing in this portrait; that in the world we know, or the world Dickens portrays, such total innocence and good humor could not amass such money.

Yet they are offered as singular mitigations in a largely dark world, and the power of the novels is mainly on the dark side. These are novels about disorder, and unseemly marriages, or the threat of unseemly marriages, are a particularly cogent indication of this disorder. The old miser Gride plots to marry the beautiful, young, and good Madeline Bray. Ralph Nickleby's marriage had been unseemly because he was a creature of money and his wife a woman of heart and flesh. The Mantalinis are a reversal of an old convention — a handsome unfaithful man who preys on and lives off his unattractive, infatuated wife. And at one point in this story, it appears that Mrs. Nickleby is considering a second marriage, to the amorous, elderly idiot who lives on the other side of the garden wall and throws tributes of cucumbers and marrows over to her.

Crime is another evidence of disorder, again indicating social as well as individual aberration. There are many criminals in *Nicholas Nickleby*: Brooker, Ralph Nickleby's former clerk, whom he had used for his dirty work and then abandoned — and who then, for revenge, kidnapped Nickleby's son and put him to board with Squeers under the false name of Smike; Squeers, too, who really conspires to make away with boys; Snawley, who swears for a fee that Smike is his son, in order that he may be taken from his friends and destroyed; Ralph Nickleby himself, who, in addition to his dishonest business practices, invites Sir Mulberry Hawk to kill Nicholas, and tries to destroy Smike in order to injure Nicholas.

The plot against Smike is foiled, but he dies nevertheless of an incurable disease that is the direct result of his early bad treatment. This premature death is also a sign of disorder but of a disorder that goes finally beyond social control. There is a groping here toward tragic disorder, but the death itself is a reconciliation, an assertion of final order:

He fell into a light slumber, and waking smiled as before; then, spoke of beautiful gardens, which he said stretched out before him, and were filled with figures of men, women, and many children, all with light upon their faces; then, whispered that it was Eden — and so died.

The Old Curiosity Shop presents variations on the same themes in a vein that is both more fanciful and more limited. Again we have the disfigurements of money, chiefly in the characters of Quilp and Little Nell's grandfather. Among Dickens' usurers, Quilp is an advance in violence even over Ralph Nickleby. He is a sadist, and usury is one instrument of his sadism. He means to make victims of those who borrow money from him. Little Nell's grandfather is a gambler who ruins himself through the pitiful delusion that by assiduous or industrious gambling he can multiply his fortune and gain financial security for Nell. It is not the love of gambling itself that moves him, but, ironically, a terrible, delusive impulse toward safety.

Again, neither government nor institutions afford any protection to the innocent against the devices of Quilp or the psychotic irresponsibility of Nell's grandfather. The law, most of the time it is in evidence, reinforces the wicked in their assault on the innocent through the corrupt efforts of the two attorneys Brass, brother and sister. Industry too is a corruptive force, as Little Nell and her grandfather discover when they wander through an industrial area, described in terms that anticipate *Hard Times*. The only evident recourse, and an unpredictable one, is once more individual benevolence. The wanderings of Little Nell and her grandfather make for opportunity to introduce a number of benefactors. The girl and old man are harbored on different occasions by Mrs. Jarley, owner of a wax-work museum, by an old forge-tender who is an amateur philosopher, and finally by a monastic schoolteacher. Little Nell's friend Kit profits from the benevolence of the eccentric rubicund Garland family, another set of Cheerybles. And Nell's granduncle, returned to England rich and forgiving after years abroad, would be a final benefactor to Nell and to his brother, but fails to find them in time, a failure that perhaps has general significance.

The trenchant signs of disorder are in this novel, too. There is the unseemly marriage of the evil dwarf Quilp to a young, pretty wife whom he denies and torments. The actions of Quilp and his associates move over increasingly from the shady to the criminal, and toward the end, when justice is at last about to catch up with the dwarf and even his associates have betrayed him, Quilp dies in the river while trying to escape — a death remarkably reminiscent of Bill Sikes's death in *Oliver Twist*, and anticipating the retributive use of the river in *Our Mutual Friend*.

The death of the young and innocent Little Nell is the climax of *The Old Curiosity Shop*, a climax prepared for by the parallel death earlier in the novel of the old schoolmaster's favorite pupil. Little Nell's death is neither accidental nor unpreventable, but the result of the deprivation and wear imposed on her by poverty, injustice, and ill-usage. But once more in death there is reconciliation: "No sleep so beautiful and calm, so free from trace of pain, so fair to look upon. She seemed a creature fresh from the hand of God, and waiting for the breath of life; not one who had lived and suffered death."

Barnaby Rudge is a historical novel having for its climactic and resolving action the anti-Catholic riots of 1780 known as the Gordon riots. The book has obvious affinities with *A Tale of Two Cities*. Both are stories of violent insurrection in which the burden of judgment opposes violence, but there is nonetheless considerable illumination of the way social injustice makes the under-privileged and down-trodden prone to violence.

In this historical context, the usual themes, though present, are not treated in the same proportion that they are in the other, more nearly contemporary novels of this period. Primary emphasis is given to the insufficiency of government to deal with the misery of the poor, and the dangers this creates. Most pointed, perhaps, is the story of Hugh the ostler, who becomes one of the chief rioters on no principle at all, but only to revenge himself on society. Hugh's mother had been hanged in his sight at Tyburn when he was only a child of six, for some minor theft of bread to feed herself and her starving child, who was the bastard son of a nobleman who had taken her as his mistress and then deserted her. That Hugh turned out badly is scarcely matter of wonder. The wonder is only that he has a bold, fearless badness, rather than a sneaky shrewd ability for self-preservation. He has his own nobility, in fact, which is seen most clearly when, in prison, waiting to be executed, he makes an impassioned plea for the life of the innocent, feeble-minded Barnaby. The burden of significance of Hugh's story is clear: that poverty and injustice make evil men out of the potentially noble.

The government does little to prevent the causes of riot and does almost as little to quell the riot when it first starts. What could have been squelched by firm action at the outset snowballs to great proportions because of the failure of the timid unknowing magistrates to act with decision. Finally the riots can be halted only with great bloodshed. The inadequacy and irrationality of the law is burlesqued through the character of the hangman, Dennis, one of the boldest rioters at the storming of Newgate until, remembering that he is a hangman, he does not wish to free the prisoners in the death cells and thereby deprive his profession of work. To the other rioters, who wish to free them and do, he says: "Don't you know they're left for death on Thursday? Don't you respect the law — the constitootion — nothing?"

Again criminality is explored, and unseemly marriages, and again this is a world in which the young and innocent can die. There is ruddy benevolence here, too, though not the genteel benevolence of the successful upper-middleclass businessman now, but the blunter, plainer, rougher-handed benevolence of Gabriel Varden, the locksmith, who is in the tradition of the just, hearty master artisan of Dekker and the Elizabethan realistic comedy.

Martin Chuzzlewit is more similar to *Nicholas Nickleby* than to either *The Old Curiosity Shop* or *Barnaby Rudge,* except in the broad satire of the American trip taken by Martin and Mark Tapley. But the American trip is really an interpolation, separate from the main action. The ugly, disfiguring effect of money as a social force is the central or organizing concern of this novel. Old Martin Chuzzlewit, believing that people seek him out only for his money, eventually has little or no relationship with anyone and is hard put to distinguish his true enemies from his imagined ones. Pecksniff pretends to goodness as a means to camouflage his cheating ways of making money. Jonas Chuzzlewit is so impatient to get his father's money that he tries to poison the old man in

order to hasten the process. Even for young Martin
Chuzzlewit, money has been a barrier to feeling and understanding, and it takes poverty and misfortune to hu-
manize him and teach him the value of fellow-feeling.

There is remarkably little about government or institutions in this novel, as there is little too about the poor,
unless we take Sairy Gamp as an example of the callous
brutality bred by poverty. Business — particularly big,
non-productive, speculative business, in this case a huge
bogus insurance enterprise — begins to take the weight
of satire Dickens has previously directed at government.
The benevolent rich who are a feature of the three
other novels are absent from *Chuzzlewit*, except as old
Martin himself, after he has seen the light near the end
of the book, promises to be something of this sort. There
is, however, the strange, highly energetic, penniless benevolence of Mark Tapley, who looks for unfortunate
people to whom to attach himself, because he thinks
there's no "credit in being jolly" except in the face of
adversity.

There are the customary signs of disorder, like Jonas
Chuzzlewit's marriage to Pecksniff's lively younger
daughter, Merry, only to humble her and make her suffer
for the fun she has made of him. In Dickens' imagination, usury is often accompanied by impotence — and,
peculiarly, an impotence that substitutes sadism for sexuality. When Mrs. Gamp gives the newly-wed Merry her
card, advertising her services as a midwife, the comedy is
not innocent but unpleasant, because the reader somehow knows that with Jonas as her husband, Merry will
have no need of a midwife. Jonas, like Quilp, is a man
who does not even spend his nights in bed. Crime and

criminality too are prominent. In addition to the insuramce fraud, very nearly a topical reference, there is Jonas Chuzzlewit's attempt to poison his father and his murder of Montague.

So in varying ways and to varying extents, but without disabling repetition, all four of these novels employ the same themes, themes, moreover, that are not idiosyncratic — though their treatment may be — but can be given added application by the experience of any reader. This centrality of his themes has much to do with Dickens' great popularity as well as with his special claim to be a realist. In *Dombey and Son* and the novels that follow, the same themes are present, but in a new state of coherence, in a higher order of relationship to each other. At its best, this is a coherence of balance between the stringent purposefulness of *Oliver Twist* and the highly relaxed excursioning of *The Pickwick Papers*.

Chapter Four

THE SENSE OF SOCIETY

By the mid 1840's, Dickens' literary ambition had grown both greater and more certain in its objects. He had two accounts to make in his fiction: one of himself, and another of the world in which he lived. No objects could be less recondite. Nor of course are they exclusive. Yet the emphasis differs plainly. In two books, *David Copperfield* and *Great Expectations*, Dickens tries to place himself in his world; in *Dombey and Son*, *Bleak House*, *Little Dorrit*, and *Our Mutual Friend*, he assesses the world in which he finds himself and condemns its deficiencies. *Hard Times*, *A Tale of Two Cities*, and *The Mystery of Edwin Drood*, though obviously products of the same genius and preoccupations, are special books that cannot be fitted into either of these categories without violence.

In *Dombey and Son*, *Bleak House*, *Little Dorrit* and *Our Mutual Friend*, a unique genre of social fiction is evolved with progressive certainty. As in such earlier novels as *Oliver Twist* and *Nicholas Nickleby*, focal attack is made on single ills. But in the later books, these ills always have a rich symbolic potential. Most simply, the Chancery of *Bleak House* or the Marshalsea of *Little Dorrit* stands for far more than does the ragged school of

Nicholas Nickleby or the poor house of *Oliver Twist.* In addition, immediate social ills are always set now in a larger context of possibility and limitation, developed at least as carefully and densely. The means employed to render this context are again symbolic, and the symbols are uniformly naturalistic and immediate — the river, the sea, the fog, the plague, the railroad. When the method, then, is at its most successful, the different materials merge: the symbols that are also natural facts, and the facts that have symbolic overtones, are the same fabric.

Whatever the conscious or careless anachronisms employed, these were contemporary novels meant to bear so tellingly and precisely on their own time that no reader could escape the burden of their vision. Yet that they retain their power to move and engage the mind a hundred years later and in different places, makes it clear that topical suggestion, though their necessary beginning, is only that. If a hundred years had not obfuscated the extent to which topical materials are used in these novels, it is certain that much that is now generally considered invention would be recognized as literal fact. Yet no simple reflection of their immediate world, no matter how vivid, could account for the way these novels survive that immediate world so nearly entire. The inexhaustible question then has to do with what makes these novels art — with how they offer that pleasure that history cannot give.

DOMBEY AND SON

Though there is a marked increase in severity of tone and treatment from *Dombey and Son,* to *Bleak House,* to *Little Dorrit*, to *Our Mutual Friend*, basically the vision of the world is constant. Indeed, the world of *Dombey and Son* scarcely admits any possibility of deterioration:

Alas! are there so few things in the world, about us, most unnatural, and yet most natural in being so? Hear the magistrate or judge admonish the unnatural outcasts of society; unnatural in brutal habits, unnatural in want of decency, unnatural in losing and confounding all distinctions between good and evil; unnatural in ignorance, in vice, in recklessness, in contumacy, in mind, in looks, in everything. But follow the good clergyman or doctor, who, with his life imperilled at every breath he draws, goes down into their dens, lying within the echoes of our carriage wheels and daily tread upon the pavement stones. Look round upon the world of odious sights — millions of immortal creatures have no other world on earth — at the lightest mention of which humanity revolts, and dainty delicacy, living in the next street, stops her ears, and lisps "I don't believe it!" Breathe the polluted air, foul with every impurity that is poisonous to health and life; and have every sense, conferred upon our race for its delight and happiness, offended, sickened and disgusted, and made a channel by which misery and death alone can enter. Vainly attempt to think of any single plant, or flower, or wholesome weed, that, set in this foetid bed, could have its natural growth, or put its little leaves off to the sun as God designed it. And then, calling up some ghastly child, with stunted form and wicked face, hold forth on its unnatural sinfulness, and lament its being, so early, far away from Heaven — but think a little of its having been conceived, and born and bred, in Hell!

The world of all these novels is a hell in which nature has been corrupted, and un-nature has become the rule.

Dickens' friend and biographer John Forster wrote that by its author's intention *Dombey and Son* "was to

do with Pride what . . . [*Martin Chuzzlewit*] had done
with Selfishness." [1] Forster then quickly added that the
novel as executed went far beyond these original intentions. Actually, it is hard to find in *Dombey and Son*
any precise equivalent for the fog-Chancery theme in
Bleak House, the imprisonment theme in *Little Dorrit*,
the money-dust theme in *Our Mutual Friend*. What Dombey himself suffers from is a monomania of which perverse pride is only a contributing part. It is his monomania that distorts the natural and makes law of the unnatural, and from it proceeds all the governable ruin of
the story — as distinguished, that is, from the immitigable
fact of man's mortality.

The notion of monomania is explicit in the initial description of Dombey, and the relation of his monomania
to the distortion of nature:

And again he said "Dom-bey and Son," in exactly the same
tone as before.

Those three words conveyed the one idea of Mr. Dombey's
life. The earth was made for Dombey and Son to trade in, and
the sun and moon were made to give them light. Rivers and
seas were formed to float their ships; rainbows gave them
promise of fair weather; winds blew for or against their
enterprises; stars and planets circled in their orbits, to preserve
inviolate a system of which they were the centre. Common
abbreviations took new meanings in his eyes, and had sole
reference to them: A. D. had no concern with anno Domini,
but stood for anno Dombei — and Son.

The picture is then built up further: "Dombey and Son had
often dealt in hides, but never in hearts"; or, Dombey
"had a sense within him, that if his wife should sicken

[1] *Life of Charles Dickens,* VI, 2.

and decay, he would be very sorry, and that he would find a something gone from among his plate and furniture, and other household possessions, which was well worth the having, and could not be lost without sincere regret. Though it would be a cool, business-like, gentlemanly, self-possessed regret, no doubt." Even after the death of Paul, Dombey thinks of "this lost child, who was to have divided with him his riches, and his projects, and his power, and allied with whom he was to have shut out all the world as with a double door of gold."

Of course this is a vicious delusion. Money can have a cruel power over life — Dombey can, for example, deny Mrs. Toodles her family, and send Walter Gay to the East Indies to die. But the ultimate efficacy of money — Paul Dombey's question: What can money really do? — is problematical. The good-hearted and simpleminded Captain Cuttle and Mr. Toots are eager to give away their money. Mrs. Skewton and good Mrs. Brown, however, are of Dombey's persuasion that money can do anything. In time, though, they, and Dombey too, must learn at least that the order of money and business is no order for human relations.

The stories of Mrs. Skewton and her daughter Edith, and good Mrs. Brown and her daughter Alice, are parallel stories. The girls look very much alike, are cousins, and suffer similar fates despite the vast class and financial differences between them. The parallelism is perhaps too mechanical, so that when Alice, explaining to Harriet Carker how her mother brought her up, says that no lady ever brought her daughter up this way, and that "the only instances of mothers bringing up their daughters wrong, and evil coming of it, are among such miserable

folk as us," the dramatic irony is gross. The point, of
course, is that each of these mothers has regarded her
beautiful daughter as a business asset, and each of these
unnatural upbringings precipitates disaster. Against this,
there is special meaningfulness in Florence Dombey's
pleasure that Walter Gay marries her when she is homeless and penniless.

For Dickens, never reconciled to his own abused childhood, ideas of nurture, fostering, and education were always important; and the different relations of parent and
quasi-parent to child, starting with that of Dombey to
his two children, are played off against each other in
great detail. The way Dombey's monomania destroys his
relationship not only with the child he hates but also with
the one he thinks he loves is altogether clear. Sol Gills,
as foster-father to Walter, shows what a natural father
should be, and the Toodles family also serve as examples
of what natural parents may do. The only bad number
in the Toodles family is Rob the Grinder, who is a condemnation not of his parents but of an unnatural education that comes to him through the businesslike offices of
Dombey.

The school, which stands *in loco parentis*, is similarly
regarded. So we have the unnatural Grinders' school and
the Blimbers' school, too, which is just as unnatural:

The Doctor [Blimber] only undertook the charge of ten
young gentlemen, but he had, always ready, a supply of learning for a hundred, on the lowest estimate; and it was at once
the business and delight of his life to gorge the unhappy ten
with it.

In fact, Doctor Blimber's establishment was a great hot-
house, in which there was a forcing apparatus incessantly at
work. All the boys blew before their time.

Mrs. Pipchin too, as a kind of teacher-parent, is all that such a person should not be — mean, unloving, selfish, cruel. It is Florence, who loves Paul, who is both his best teacher and his best parent.

Love, not business, is the only basis for human relationships, but actually not even business itself can be conducted as Dombey conducts Dombey and Son without disaster. For Dombey values a dignified appearance equally over the real situation of his marriage and the solvency of his firm. The attack in *Dombey and Son* is not really on business at all, but on a poor outmoded kind of business mentality that carries its standards over into areas where they are even less useful and more ruinous than they are in business. Of business and industrial progress as such Dickens is at least tolerant. Though Sol Gills can make nothing from his antiquated instrument business, he does well when he anticipates the direction of progress, and makes some good investments; and the railroad, though its ugly potentialities are seen, is regarded chiefly as an instrument of progress, that helps clear slums, and gives the stoker, Mr. Toodles, a dignified independence. Only in Dombey's reactionary imagination is the railway regarded as Death.

Yet Carker's death gives symbolic justice to Dombey's delusion; and there is final justification, too, for the end of all progress is certainly death. Death is the summary fact of life: "The old, old fashion! The fashion that came in with our first garments, and will last unchanged until our race has run its course, and the wide firmament is rolled up like a scroll." Dickens tells us that there is "that older fashion yet, of Immortality," but in his own imagination it is not immortality but death that is an awful, swelling, almost constant presence. It is death that mocks and makes hollow nonsense of prides and mono- manias, distorted and unnatural orders of conduct, busi- nesslike failures in love and fellow-feeling. In *Dombey and Son*, quite clearly, death — the great common bond between all men — is the covert controlling theme, the reality against which the unnatural distortions of life are measured and discovered for what they are. That it was so meant, from the beginning, is clear in Dickens' notes for the novel. An early note on Paul, for example, reads: "Boy born to die." Paul seems really to have one foot in the grave at birth, and it is this which gives him his power to pierce false appearance and delusion — makes him, as Dickens says again in his notes, an "old child."

Death is the great sea into which the river of life flows, and for which it is intended from its source. The figure is obsessive in Dickens' imagination, comes almost in- evitably when he writes of death, and seems never to lose its freshness or terrible force. When the first Mrs. Dombey dies with Florence in her arms:

The Doctor gently brushed the scattered ringlets of the child aside from the face and mouth of the mother. Alas how calm they lay there; how little breath there was to stir them!

Thus, clinging fast to that slight spar within her arms, the mother drifted out upon the dark and unknown sea that rolls round all the world.

It is remarkable here how the sea image is anticipated even before it is properly invoked, by the ringlets on the mother's mouth, "calm," and "with little breath to stir them," almost like sails on a becalmed sea.

One afternoon Paul takes a nap on the seashore, while
Florence watches him. Suddenly he awakens, startled:

> Florence asked him what he thought he heard.
> "I want to know what it says," he answered, looking steadily
> in her face. "The sea, Floy, what is it that it keeps on saying?"
> She told him that it was only the noise of the rolling waves.
> "Yes, yes," he said. "But I know that they are always say-
> ing something. Always the same thing. What place is over
> there?" He rose up, looking eagerly at the horizon.
> She told him that there was another country opposite, but
> he said he didn't mean that: he meant farther away — farther
> away!
> Very often afterwards, in the midst of their talk, he would
> break off, to try to understand what it was that the waves
> were always saying; and would rise up in his couch to look
> towards that invisible region, far away.

What that "invisible region" is, is scarcely ambiguous.
Talking to the Blimbers about the porter Glubb, Paul
says that Glubb knows a great deal about the sea, but
"don't know why the sea should make me think of my
Mama that's dead." Or again, Mr. Toots, who befriends
Paul at the Blimbers', goes to visit him in his room one
evening, and finds him staring through the window at a
vision of a boat on the waves that seems to beckon him to
come.
When Paul is actually dying, he repeatedly visions and
is troubled by "the swift and rapid river"; "that rushing
river. Why will it never stop, Floy? . . . It is bearing me
away, I think"; "the dark, dark river rolled towards the
sea in spite of him"; "the river running very fast, and
confusing his mind." And at the end:

"Now lay me down," he said, "and, Floy, come close to me and let me see you!"

Sister and brother wound their arms around each other, and the golden light came streaming in, and fell upon them, locked together.

"How fast the river runs, between its green banks and the rushes, Floy! But it's very near the sea. I hear the waves! They always said so!"

Presently he told her that the motion of the boat upon the stream was lulling him to rest. How green the banks were now, how bright the flowers growing on them, and how tall the rushes! Now the boat was out at sea, but gliding smoothly on. And now there was a shore before him. Who stood on the bank! —

He put his hands together, as he had been used to do at his prayers. He did not remove his arms to do it; but they saw him fold them so, behind her neck.

"Mama is like you, Floy. I know her by the face! But tell them that the print upon the stairs at school is not divine enough. The light about the head is shining on me as I go!"

The golden ripple on the wall came back again, and nothing else stirred in the room. The old, old fashion! The fashion that came in with our first garments, and will last unchanged until our race has run its course, and the wide firmament is rolled up like a scroll. The old, old fashion — Death!

Oh thank God, all who see it, for that older fashion yet, of Immortality! And look upon us, angels of young children, with regards not quite estranged, when the swift river bears us to the ocean!

Later, whenever Florence looks at the river, she thinks with "awful wonder" of the river "her brother had so often said was bearing him away." And in her dreams

Paul tells her that the river "is running on . . . has never stopped," and that she is "moving with it."

The sea is the constant fact of time. All goes on "as it was wont. The waves are hoarse with repetition of their mystery; the dust lies piled upon the shore; the sea-birds soar and hover; the winds and clouds go forth upon their trackless flight; the white arms beckon, in the moonlight, to the invisible country far away." Even Mrs. Skewton is buried at the edge of the sea, and though her friends shun her funeral, and try to pay no attention to the waves and the dust and the white arms beckoning, Edith at least stands on the edge of the sea, "alone, and listening to its waves, has dank weed cast up at her feet, to strew her path in life withal." In his notes, Dickens had written: "End with the sea — carrying through, what the waves were always saying, and the invisible country far away." [2]

All the themes of the preceding four novels are in *Dombey and Son* too: money, poverty, benevolence, unseemly marriages, criminality, death of the young. But here their connections are more apparent, and Dickens attempts to draw them into a structural complex. The initial notion of the use of pride, however, is fuzzily conceived, and even at its clearest is inadequate to support the range and complexity of the story. Dickens' view of pride is too simple, has too few of the overtones that it would have for a less secular, more Christian imagination. More resonant and useful for him is the relatively undeclared idea of death — symbolized by the con-

---

[2] The passage written to carry out this instruction to himself was cut in proof when the final number had to be reduced by seven lines. See John Butt and Kathleen Tillotson, *Dickens at Work* (London, 1957), p. 112.

stant flow of the river into the sea — as the destroyer of delusion, the teacher of truth. This use of death, with its river-sea symbolism, is present in all the novels of Dickens' maturity.

BLEAK HOUSE

In *Bleak House*, as in *Dombey and Son*, death functions as a touchstone of reality. It is a measure of the wretchedness of man's earthly sojourn, awful and profound, but — and this is much to the point — more kindly than the torments imposed by society. One of Esther Summerson's earlier memories is of a sombre birthday, the only recognition of which was her godmother's remark after dinner: "It would have been far better, little Esther, that you had had no birthday; that you had never been born!" When Caddy Jellyby gives her first confidence to Esther, her misery bursts from her uncontrollably: "I wish I was dead! . . . I wish we were all dead. It would be a great deal better for us!" The bricklayer's wife, Liz, thinking of her friend Jenny's dead baby, says: "Ah, Jenny, Jenny! . . . better so. Much better to think of dead than alive, Jenny! Much better!" And of her own child, sleeping, she says: "If he should be turned bad, 'spite of all I could do, and the time should come when I should sit by him in his sleep, made hard and changed, an't it likely I should think of him as he lies in my lap now, and wish he had died as Jenny's child died!" Mr. Jarndyce, horrified to find that Richard has based all his expectations on the outcome of the chancery suit, says: "Whatever you do on this side the grave, never give one lingering glance towards the horrible phantom that has haunted us so many years. Better to

borrow, better to beg, better to die!" Poor Mr. Jellyby
tells Caddy that she and her brothers and sisters have
been allowed to grow up like Indians, without care or
teaching, and that "the best thing that could happen to
them was, their being all Tomahawked together." Esther
again, when she discovers the secret of her parentage,
feels and knows "it would have been better and happier
for many people, if indeed I had never breathed." And
Jo, when he is caught by Allan Woodcourt and Jenny,
says: "Can't you never let such an unfortnet as me alone?
An't I unfortnet enough for you yet? How unfortnet
do you want me fur to be? I've been a chivied and a
chivied, fust by one on you and nixt by another on you,
till I'm worritted to skins and bones. The Inkwhich
warn't *my* fault. *I* done nothink. He wos wery good to
me, he wos; he was the only one I knowed to speak to,
as ever come across my crossing. It ain't wery likely I
should want him to be Inkwhich'd. I only wish I wos,
myself. I don't know why I don't go and make a hole in
the water, I'm sure I don't."

Jo is an extreme example of a recurrent type in Dickens' novels: the child already old with knowledge of the
ways and miseries of the world. Guppy and Smallweed
are repellent examples of the same type. But Jo, a far
more extreme version, though repellent too, also stirs our
compassion. Among many other things, Jo knows about
dying. When Charley tells him he shouldn't sleep at the
brick kiln, because people die there, he says: "They dies
everywheres . . . They dies more than they lives, according to what *I* see." And when it comes Jo's time to die,
the fears he has are not of death. His only fear is of being
taken back to Tom-All-Alone's. He thinks of death as

being "moved on as fur as ever I could go and couldn't
be moved no furdur." It is peace for him, quiet, the end
of the need to move on. Just before the end he starts up,
afraid that he will not get to the paupers' burying ground
in time — or that, once there, he will not be allowed to
get in, that they will not unlock it for him. But at last:

The light is come upon the dark benighted way. Dead!
Dead, your Majesty. Dead, my lords and gentlemen. Dead,
Right Reverends and Wrong Reverends of every order. Dead,
men and women, born with Heavenly compassion in your
hearts. And dying thus around us every day.

Jo is a central character in *Bleak House*. He might,
in fact, be called *the* central character. In his notes for
Chapter XXIX, Dickens wrote: "Then connect Esther
and Jo." And by one means or another, Jo is "connected"
with virtually all the characters of importance in *Bleak
House*. This is not accident, nor even the storymaker's
simple and inevitable extension of coincidence to tie his
story together. The notes to *Bleak House* begin with several lists of possible titles for the novel. Every list but the
final and deciding one starts with the title "Tom-All-
Alone's." And in his notes for Chapter XVI, Dickens
indicated that Tom-All-Alone's was "the ruined property
in Jarndyce and Jarndyce, already described by Mr.
Jarndyce."

Mr. Jarndyce does describe the property which he pro-
phesies quite correctly will no longer be anything but
the means to pay the lawyers' costs in the case. "It is a
street of perishing blind houses, with their eyes stoned
out; without a pane of glass, without so much as a win-
dow-frame, with the bare blank shutters tumbling from

their hinges and falling asunder; the iron rails peeling
away in flakes of rust; the chimneys sinking in; the stone
steps to every door (and every door might be Death's
Door) turning stagnant green; the very crutches on
which the ruins are propped, decaying. These are the
Great Seal's impressions . . . all over England — the
children know them!"

Dickens is vehement against that moneyed world of
fashion which is "wrapped up in too much jeweller's cotton and fine wool, and cannot hear the rushing of the
larger worlds, and cannot see them as they circle round
the sun." He insists that this ignorance does not just be-
fall the well-to-do but that it is actually willed by them,
that part of the *status quo* they wish to preserve is the
status quo of their own ignorance, the peculiar ignorance
of "ladies and gentlemen . . . who have agreed to put a
smooth glaze on the world, and to keep down all its
realities. . . . Who have found out the perpetual stoppage."

Such a "perpetual stoppage" is, of course, as impossible
as Dombey's "double door of gold" to "shut out all the
world." Truth has terrible ways to assert itself, and not
even wealth, though it has many protections, is a barrier to infection. Tom-All-Alone's will have its revenge.
"Even the winds are his messengers, and they serve him
in these hours of darkness. There is not a drop of Tom's
corrupted blood but propagates infection and contagion
somewhere. It shall pollute, this very night, the choice
stream . . . of a Norman house, and his Grace shall not
be able to say Nay to the infamous alliance. There is not
an atom of Tom's slime, not a cubic inch of any pestilen-
tial gas in which he lives, not one obscenity or degradation about him, not an ignorance, not a wickedness, not

a brutality of his committing, but shall work its retribution, through every order of society, up to the proudest
of the proud, and to the highest of the high. Verily,
what with tainting, plundering, and spoiling, Tom has
his revenge." Jo carries his fever about with him as he is
hounded around the country. Charley catches it from
him, and Esther Summerson catches it from Charley.
They have been kind to Jo, but the realist Dickens knows
that the fruits of social injustice are not distributed in
any strict accordance with deserving. And at Jo's bed-
side, when he is dying, both Mr. Jarndyce and Allan
Woodcourt think "how strangely Fate has entangled this
rough outcast in the web of very different lives."

Epidemic is nature's counterpart for revolution. In
Dickens' mind, disease and oppression were closely
linked. In 1854, the year after he finished *Bleak House*,
he warned Lady Burdett-Coutts of the danger the government faced if it did not take proper measures to control cholera:

Let it [the cholera] come twice again, severely, — the people
advancing all the while in the knowledge that, humanly speaking, it is, like Typhus Fever in the mass, a preventible disease
— and you will see such a shake in this country as never was
seen on Earth since Sampson pulled the Temple down upon
his head.[3]

The misery that makes people long for death also and
similarly breeds violence. By this time in the fifties, revolution seemed a dreadful and present possibility to Dickens. It is surely the possibility that lurks in the fog and
mire of *Bleak House*.

When Richard asks Krook why his shop is called

[3] *Coutts Letters*, p. 273.

Chancery, the old man starts to explain directly; then is
diverted by Ada's hair, and says he has three sacks of
ladies' hair below in his shop; then finally does explain
that he and the Lord Chancellor "both grub on in a mud-
dle." By this time and through his inadvertence, we suspect what the human consequences of this grubbing and
muddling are. When Krook dissolves of spontaneous
combustion, Dickens tells us that this is the death "of all
Lord Chancellors in all Courts, and of all authorities in
all places under all names soever, where false pretenses
are made, and where injustice is done . . . [a death] in-
born, inbred, engendered in the corrupted humours of
the vicious body itself."

A kind of inevitable dissolution is the hope, but how
much is invested in this hope? Wll the Dedlocks (surely
the name is symbolic: dead-lock) break up or must they
be broken up? Toward the end of *Bleak House* it is the
suit of Jarndyce and Jarndyce that "lapses and melts
away," but not Chancery, and it is clear that Dickens has
grave doubts that enough will happen by peaceful process. When Esther and Ada visit the bricklayers' house
with Mrs. Pardiggle, they both feel "painfully sensible
that between us and these people there [is] an iron barrier." Miss Flite, who in her own flighty way is a social
realist too, expects a judgment on the Day of Judgment
when she will release or give flight to those birds, Hope,
Joy, etc., which symbolize all that is frustrate and im-
prisoned in the hell of the world. Mr. Boythorn says
that the only possible way to reform Chancery is to blow
it to atoms "with ten thousand hundred-weight of gun-
powder," and in the next instant he calls Sir Leicester
Dedlock "the most stiff-necked, arrogant, imbecile, pig-

headed numskull, ever, by some inexplicable mistake of Nature, born in any station of life but a walking-stick's."

It is the obduracy of the old bad system that makes the hope for gradual or peaceful improvement seem so small to Dickens — this obduracy, and terrible ignorance too, for the fog and mire of *Bleak House* are the fog and mire of ignorance. The willful ignorance of the upper classes is based on a limited concept of self-interest; but middle-class ignorance is something else. Mr. Turvey-drop — in whose name the dropping that is a bow or curtsey and the dropping that is animal excrement become inextricably combined — is a genteelly impoverished and hypocritical worshipper of the upper classes, a gentlemen's gentleman, part of that middle class that Dickens describes as no class at all, but only a fringe on the mantle of the upper class. Mr. Bayham Badger, another member of this no-class, prides himself ridiculously on the gentility of his wife's former husbands.

This pretentious ignorance, amounting to a failure of self-interest, is specially galling to Dickens, for he feels that there is nothing to hope from a man who fails to recognize even his own needs and reasonable claims, whose pretensions cause him to be ignorant of his own interests. In this cataloguing of kinds of ignorance, there is the self-deluding ignorance too of the Mrs. Jellybys and Mrs. Pardiggles, who find it easier to do good deeds at a distance than to do their duty close by. And there is Krook, who has his own brand of ignorance — the stubborn, self-destroying, and vicious but still comic ignorance of craft — and won't ask anyone to teach him to read because they might teach him wrong.

The most dangerous ignorance of all, though, is the ignorance of those too down-trodden in the world to know or care. A couple of years later, Dickens was to tell a friend that "the alienation of the people from their own public affairs" was "extremely like the general mind of France before the breaking out of the first Revolution." [4] To every question addressed to him, Jo says "*I don't know nothink* [no-think?]." Dickens compares Jo to a vagabond dog, and says: "Turn that dog's descendants wild . . . and in a very few years they will so degenerate that they will lose even their bark — but not their bite." The logic of the drama scarcely requires Dickens' explanation.

Bleak House confronts authority — the authority of office, and of money, and of family — with the misery of the world. Mr. Gridley asks who is responsible, and Esther tells Mr. Skimpole that she fears "everybody is obliged to be" responsible. Responsibility is part of Esther Summerson's great and revolting virtue. Most of the other impossible young women in Dickens' novels spring from the usual source for perfect young women in fiction, the area of erotic wish-fulfillment. But Esther stirs no chord of desire, and it is more likely that Dickens has created her as some kind of *alter ego* for himself, deprived of his aggressive force and talent but made kind and lovable instead. Lovable, too, for herself — not for her beauty, which for a time she loses, nor for her wealth and influence, which she never has. She starts as an unloved child, as Dickens at least fancied that he was himself, and there are certain aspects of her childhood that remind us of Pip and David Copperfield, the only

[4] *Letters* II, 651, to Layard, 10 April 1855.

other first-person narrators in Dickens' novels, and each
in some sense a self-portrait. But Dickens had to take
back all that he thought the world owed him for his lost
childhood, and more, by the force of his own hand,
whereas everything comes back to Esther Summerson
through love. Yet it requires none of this speculation to
see that Esther has a schematic place in the novel by
being responsible: as John Jarndyce is, as Charley is,
as Mrs. Bagnet is, as Allan Woodcourt is, as Bucket is,
as the Rouncewell family are; and as Skimpole, and Mrs.
Jellyby, and Mrs. Pardiggle, and Mr. Chadband are not.
As Sir Leicester Dedlock is only by his own insufficient
lights.

The attack on Chancery, and on the law and legal
process, is an attack on irresponsibility. The law, we are
told, takes no responsibility for anything but itself. Its
first principle is "to make business for itself." It makes
hypocritical claims, of course, to much more: Mr. Tulk-
inghorn talks of his devotion to Sir Leicester Dedlock,
and Vholes talks always of putting his shoulder to the
wheel, and of his responsibility to his growing daughters, and to his old father in the Vale of Taunton. But all
this is mere sham, and what the legal gentlemen really
intend is to enrich and dignify themselves. There are, too,
many kinds of responsibility. Attractive responsibilities
are easy, but it is the unattractive ones that are the real
test. The poor, Dickens knows and shows, are unattractive, like Jo:

Dirty, ugly, disagreeable to all the senses, in body a common
creature of the common streets . . . Homely filth begrimes him,
homely parasites devour him, homely sores are in him, homely
rags are on him: native ignorance, the growth of English soil

and climate, sinks his immortal nature lower than the beasts that perish. Stand forth, Jo, in uncompromising colours! From the sole of thy foot to the crown of thy head, there is nothing interesting about thee.

It is easy to be responsible for pretty Rosa, or rosy Mrs. Rouncewell. But who will be responsible for Jo, or for Nemo, the wretched nobody that Captain Hawdon becomes after he has failed in responsibility. For Esther's illegitimacy too is regarded in the light of responsibility, not of sexual morality, and both her father and her mother are made to pay a final price for their irresponsibility toward her.

The very point being made, and that helps substantiate this novel's realism, is that responsibility is difficult, indirect, often very obscure, but that the price of irresponsibility must be paid nonetheless. This is conveyed obviously by the fog-law analogy; less obviously but perhaps more tellingly by the indirect exactions made by disease, epidemic. Only when we have paid the price for our irresponsibilities — secret or unclear as they may be — can we "begin the world." Chancery is the set theme of this novel, death is the reality against which the foggy irresponsibility of legal process is assessed, and epidemic — moving by terrible indirection — symbolizes all too realistically the disaster that continued irresponsibility will bring.

LITTLE DORRIT

If the major theme of *Little Dorrit* is imprisonment,[5] an only less general and perhaps more complicated and

[5] Lionel Trilling, in his Introduction to the Oxford Illustrated Edition of *Little Dorrit* (1953), has shown how pervasive and varied is the imprisonment imagery of this novel.

even more meaningful theme has to do with the ambiguous distinction between reality and illusion. A central place in the novel, both physically and intellectually, is occupied by Amy Dorrit's inability to find her life in Venice substantial:

> Such people were not realities to the little figure of the English girl; such people were all unknown to her. She would watch the sunset, in its long low lines of purple and red, and its burning flush high up into the sky: so glowing on the buildings, and so lightening their structure, that it made them look as if their strong walls were transparent, and they shone from within. She would watch those glories expire; and then, after looking at the black gondolas underneath, taking guests to music and dancing, would raise her eyes to the shining stars. Was there no party of her own, in other times, on which the stars had shone? To think of that old gate now!
>
> She would think of that old gate, and of herself sitting at it in the dead of night, pillowing Maggy's head; and of other places and of other scenes associated with those different times. And then she would lean upon her balcony, and look over at the water, as though they all lay underneath it. When she got to that, she would musingly watch its running, as if, in the general vision, it might run dry, and show her the prison again, and herself, and the old room, and the old inmates, and the old visitors: all lasting realities that had never changed.

"In this crowning unreality" of Venice, a city "where all the streets [are] paved with water," Amy not only fails to believe in what she sees, but begins even to doubt that the reality she once knew, in the Marshalsea prison for debtors, can really exist any more without her. Venice is the culmination of her European tour, during which, "sitting opposite her father in the travelling-carriage, and

recalling the old Marshalsea room, her present existence
was a dream. All that she saw was new and wonderful,
but it was not real"; and "even the old mean Marshalsea
was shaken to its foundations, when she pictured it without her father." Often, however, "at posting-houses, and
other halting places," beggars would approach her for
money, and "these miserable creatures would appear to
her the only realities of the day." For in the struggle or
wrestling match between misery and magnificence, misery always throws "magnificence with the strength of
fate."

We are back then to Dickens' prime reality — misery.
Misery is the palpable reality and magnificence is unreal.
The aura that surrounds money is unreal, and money itself can be illusory and filthy. Behind the name of
Merdle, the swindler, the French word for excrement
is only feebly concealed, and this analogy between money
and ordure is amplified in *Our Mutual Friend*.

William Dorrit, despite his pretenses, really shares his
daughter's difficulties. None of his new wealth and
grandeur sits naturally on him, and when he suffers the
stroke that precedes his death, at Mrs. Merdle's dinner
party, his old real life reasserts itself. He imagines himself back in the Snuggery of the Marshalsea, and believes
the fashionable assemblage to be his fellow prisoners. He
calls for Amy to come to him, and to fetch the turn-
key Bob from the lock, to help him up the narrow stairs
to his room. Amy gets him outside, pretending to look
for Bob, and into a coach and home:

The broad stairs of his Roman palace were contracted in
his failing sight to the narrow stairs of his London prison; and
he would suffer no one but her to touch him, his brother ex-

cepted. They got him up to his room without help, and laid him down on his bed. And from that hour his poor maimed spirit, only remembering the place where it had broken its wings, cancelled the dream through which it had since groped, and knew of nothing beyond the Marshalsea. When he heard footsteps in the street, he took them for the old weary tread in the yards. When the hour came for locking up, he supposed all strangers to be excluded for the night.

He goes on for ten days so before he dies, sure that he is poor again, and unable to eat the expensive invalid foods brought him because he is sure he cannot afford them until Amy pretends to pawn his watch, sleeve-buttons, and finger rings to pay for them.

The reality of William Dorrit himself hides behind a further illusion, the illusion of his disinterested character and good breeding. The benign-looking Father of the Marshalsea is really a mock-upper-class parasite, who takes anything he can get from Amy and his fellow prisoners, and does not choose to see the privations he causes them. The Patriarch Mr. Casby, another fatherly-looking figure, forces his clerk, Pancks, to screw his poor tenants in Bleeding Heart Court for their rents, while he stays at a distance from which he can enjoy the money without seeing the misery he causes. In the end, Pancks turns on Casby before his tenants and cuts off his white locks and the broad brim of his hat — a curious punishment that begs for Freudian interpretation,[6] since by this punishment the Patriarch is de-fathered.

We are dealing again, among other things, with the illusion of gentility, and the self-protecting illusions cultivated by gentility. Mrs. General, retained by Mr. Dor-

[6] As Trilling has pointed out.

rit to assist his daughters in "the formation of a surface," says that the first rule in this process is that "nothing disagreeable should ever be looked at." Government, represented by the Circumlocution Office, is gentility institutionalized. Henry Gowan, the genteel no-good who poses as a painter but more than admits he is posing, says that the Circumlocution Office is "a school for gentlemen." And this is but the beginning. The devilish Blandois justifies all he does by saying he was born to be a gentleman, and does what he has to do in order to live like one. Mr. Merdle, on whom society hangs though he is himself a misfit in society, turns out to be not a tycoon at all, but a great fraud. In a way, the meaning of what is being said is expressed in the experiences of the maid Affery, whose dreams, as she thinks or calls them, turn out to be not dreams at all but glimpses of a reality too dreadful to admit.

In the end, even Affery knows her dreams are real. All the secrets come out of disguise and the recluses out of their prisons. The invalid Mrs. Clennam, who has not left her room for years because, one infers, she cannot face the implications of her life, comes into the streets again at last, and is overwhelmed by "the want of likeness between the controllable pictures her imagination had often drawn of the life from which she was secluded, and the overwhelming rush of the reality."

Arthur Clennam finds that all his specific fears are foundless, but that there are other skeletons in his family closet that he never suspected. Similarly, Flora Finching, the childhood sweetheart whom Clennam had expected to be unchanged, is now a fat, trivial, slightly maudlin and alcoholic middle-aged woman, who speaks in a weird

stream-of-consciousness language in which appearance
and reality are hopelessly muddled. There is terrible
pathos in the divided awareness of this woman who lives
simultaneously with illusion and reality, much of the
reality of whose life is the aged malicious aunt who
comes to her on her husband's death as the chief part of
her inheritance. Here again we see Dickens' genius for
invented languages, as when Flora congratulates Amy
Dorrit on her impending marriage to Clennam:

"If Fancy's fair dreams," she began, "have ever pictured that
when Arthur — cannot overcome it pray excuse me — was
restored to freedom even a pie as far from flaky as the present
and so deficient in kidney as to be in that respect like a minced
nutmeg might not prove unacceptable if offered by the hand
of true regard such visions have forever fled and all is cancelled but being aware that tenderer relations are in contem-
plation beg to state that I heartily wish well to both and find
no fault with either not the least, it may be withering to know
that ere the hand of Time had made me much less slim than
formerly and dreadfully red on the slightest exertion particularly after eating I well know when it takes the form of a
rash it might have been and was not through the interruption
of parents and mental torpor succeeded until the mysterious
clue was held by Mr. F still I would not be ungenerous to
either and I heartily wish well to both."

It is in the Marshalsea that reality comes to Clennam,
after he has lost all his money. Here he discovers that
he loves Amy Dorrit, and it is here that she, having lost
her money too, returns to him and to reality. There can
be neither happiness nor grace, Dickens seems to be saying, except by a coming to terms with misery, that great
reality lying behind genteel illusion. It is the covert

sense of the awful reality looming behind illusion that gives this book its power; and the elaborate playing on the complex and obscure distinctions between illusion and reality lends power and vitality to the overt theme of imprisonment, even as the sea-death image vitalizes the treatment of pride in *Dombey and Son,* and the device of infection vitalizes the symbolic use of Chancery in *Bleak House.*

<h2 align="center">OUR MUTUAL FRIEND</h2>

Our Mutual Friend, Dickens' last completed novel, is the work of a great but worn genius who counteracts his loss of spontaneous powers with his accumulated resources of knowledge and craft. The novel was, as Dickens' correspondence makes clear, an agony of effort to make permanent his exacerbated vision of the world. Both his correspondence and the Memorandum Book that he kept for about eight years, starting in January 1855, indicate that he was considering certain ideas for this novel at least as early as 1861 — a long period of gestation for a writer who at the beginning of his career, at least, seemed able to start a book first and then think about it.

The plot and structure of this novel are elaborately worked out, and the thematic controls are very intricate. Central, of course, is the theme of money, in the working out of which money and dust are correlatives. In Chapter XII the wind is called a saw that blows sawdust about the city, and the bits of filthy paper that form part of this dust are "mysterious paper currency." Dust is the fact become symbol, par excellence. Dust, dust-heaps, and dust-contractors were all common in Dickens' London.

The dust collected from the streets was piled in huge heaps which came to have great value. "Jewels, coins, and other valuables were often found in them," and their more ordinary contents, "soot, cinders, broken glass, bottles, crockery, worn-out pots and pans, old paper and rags, bones, garbage, human feces, and dead cats, were picked over and sorted for sale to brickmakers, soap boilers, paper manufacturers, road makers, dealers in metal and glass, concrete makers. The soot was used as fertilizer, decayed animal and vegetable matter as manure; even the dead cats were sold for their skins."[7] A famous philanthropic dust-contractor named Henry Dodd, who was known to Dickens, gave his daughter as a wedding present a dust-heap that realized ten thousand pounds.[8]

Dickens had been somewhat aware of the exploitable symbolic potential of the dust-heaps for a long time. In *Hard Times*, Parliament is called the "national cinder-heap," where Mr. Gradgrind works at "sifting for the odds and ends he wanted, and . . . throwing of the dust about into the eyes of other people." In various of his letters, Dickens refers to Parliament as "the Great Dust Heap down at Westminster";[9] complains that the "City aristocracy . . . made such speeches and expressed such sentiments as any moderately intelligent dustman would have blushed through his cindery bloom to have thought of";[10] and castigates "a worthless Government which is afraid of every little interest and trembles before the vote of every dust contractor."[11] The first volume of *House-*

[7] Johnson, p. 1030.
[8] William Miller, "Dust Heaps," *The Dickensian*, XXXI (1935), 147–48.
[9] *Letters* II, 220–21, to Watson, 3 July 1850.
[10] *Letters* I, 517–18, to Jerrold, 3 May 1843.
[11] *Coutts Letters*, p. 273.

hold Words contains a story about the value of dust-heaps, which includes too, significantly or fortuitously, an account of how a drowning man is dragged from a canal and brought back to life.[12] The next volume also contains a piece in which dust, dust-heaps, and dustmen are prominent.[13] In *Little Dorrit*, Mrs. General inquires "what quantity of dust and ashes was deposited at the bankers'." Similar, too, is the suggestion beneath the name of Merdle, the swindling financier, of the French word "merde."

The dust-heaps were filth, ordure, excrement, but nevertheless, money; and in this elaborate working-out of how filth is considered desirable, and how men subvert their lives for it, Dickens is again on his old and inexhaustible subject of the unreality of social life. Very nearly all the main action of the novel supports and gives pertinence to the dust-money theme. There are, for example, three important marriages in *Our Mutual Friend*, between Harmon and Bella, Eugene and Lizzie, Alfred and Sophronia Lammle. In each of these marriages, money is a primary issue: Harmon, though he is or could be rich, must disguise himself and remain poor in order to be certain that Bella is not marrying him for his money; Eugene must marry Lizzie against the pressure of his family and of Society that he marry a woman with money; and the Lammles marry, each motivated solely by the delusion that the other has money. In addition to these major examples, we are told that Podsnap, who had a fortune, married another fortune; that Fledgeby's mother had to marry Fledgeby's father because

---

12 "Dust, or Ugliness Redeemed," *HW*, I (13 July 1850), 379-84.
13 "A Suburban Connemara," *HW*, II (8 March 1851), 562-65.

she could not pay back the money she had borrowed from him; that Fledgeby himself offers to pay Lammle to procure a wife for him.

Money destroys and corrupts in a wide variety of other ways, also. Old Harmon is the ruined victim of his own money. His son too is nearly ruined by this money. Boffin pretends to be corrupted by money in order to show its corruptive force, and is in fact so harassed by it that he can scarcely wait to get rid of it. Bella begins to be corrupted by money, and must be saved. Wegg is particularly susceptible to such corruption, and is corrupted. People do, or are willing to do, extraordinary things to get money. Riderhood and Hexam pick the pockets of the drowned dead — and Riderhood, occasionally, those of the living as well. Pleasant Riderhood "preys on" sailors. Mr. Dolls betrays his daughter and Lizzie for money. Riderhood agrees to become a spy for money, to withhold his knowledge of a crime for money; and he libels a dead man for money, and extorts money from the dying Betty Higden. Radfoot tries to murder, and is in turn murdered for money. The Lammles plot to gain power over well-to-do young girls in order to control and profit by their marriages. Even the good Riah plays a false role for money, although in his case it is suggested that he has little choice. Those who will stand out against the temptations of money are heroes. Lizzie would. Jenny Wren does. Wrayburn in his own way does. Bella at length does. Riah finally does. Mrs. Lammle at two points does. Venus after a time does. Sloppy and Betty Higden do. The Boffins, most notably, do.

Dickens presents education as the logical source of an alternative to money values, but a source that fails. The selfishness of Charley Hexam is fostered rather than corrected by education. Silas Wegg is a burlesque symbol of the meanness and inadequacy of education. Even the disagreeable, pretentious, and inadequate Mrs. Wilfer is a would-be school-mistress. Formal education is unnatural, unfitted to human ends. The unnaturalness of Headstone's education contributes to his downfall. The only education fitted to life is the education administered by the ignorant Boffins to Bella, or by Miss Potterson to the customers of the Six Jolly Fellowship Porters.

The home, too, has no adequacy as an instrument of education. The relations between parents and children in *Our Mutual Friend* afford not a single example of the healthy, natural, or useful. Lizzie loves and is loved by her father, to be sure, but she must prove her love by aiding him in his preying operations on the river, and for so doing she has to do guilty penance after his death. Between Hexam and his son there is only distrust. Old Harmon drives his wife and daughter to their deaths, and all but does the same to his son. Mrs. Wilfer is either a joke or a trial to her children, and Mr. Wilfer, though he loves Bella, is fully as much her child or her proxy lover as her father. Riderhood beats and derides his daughter, sets bad examples for her, and otherwise makes her life miserable. Podsnap treats his daughter as he treats his goods. Wrayburn's father, "My respected father . . . M.R.F.," "always in the clearest manner provided (as he calls it) for his children by pre-arranging from the hour of the birth of each, and sometimes from an earlier period, what the devoted little victim's calling and course in life should be." Mr. Dolls is a troublesome and crippling child to his daughter, and even her disability is made to seem a punishment for his wrongs. Fledgeby is the victim of his parents' dreadful marriage. Only foster-parents fulfill the proper functions of parents: the Boffins to John Harmon; Betty Higden to Johnny, Sloppy, and "the minders"; Riah, finally, to Jenny Wren.

Nor can government be a better parent to the people, since the House of Commons is only the "best club in London," with an initiation fee of five thousand pounds. Inevitably, then, the treatment of the poor, the moneyless, is inhumane, except at the hands of a few enlightened private philanthropic organizations, such as the Children's Hospital in London. The governing class is hopeless. The Veneerings and the Podsnaps are not governors, but only mean-spirited creatures of money. Such aristocratic vestiges as remain are either old and feeble like Twemlow, or young and feeble like Wrayburn and Lightwood. With these characters, and with Wrayburn in particular, Dickens adds a new dimension to the conventionally comic picture of the effete aristocrat, and to the consideration of class in English fiction. When the aristocracy can no longer maintain and reproduce itself, the empire must follow the path of the Roman Empire before it. It is not chance that Dickens has Wegg read Gibbon's *Decline and Fall* to Boffin. The picture of a Wrayburn too careless even to protect himself is far more prophetically terrifying than anything of the same order Firbank or Waugh will produce in the next century. And though the marriage of Wrayburn and Lizzie suggests the classic union of the lower and upper classes against the middle, Dickens offers it neither as a cure nor even as much of a hope.

By the organizing use of his social themes, then, Dickens suggests a ghastly total world. Yet these thematic repetitions in themselves, whatever their accumulation, cannot alone account for the peculiar power that this novel attains, as in Jenny Wren's eerie fancy upon the roof of Pubsey & Co., in the heart of London's financial district, that up here in the air she is happily dead:

"Oh, so tranquil!" cried the little creature, smiling. "Oh, so peaceful and so thankful! And you hear the people who are alive, crying, and working, and calling to one another down in the close dark streets, and you seem to pity them so! And such a chain has fallen from you, and such a strange good sorrowful happiness comes upon you."

Behind the apparent anarchy of society, there is the constancy of death and dying, Paul Dombey's "old fashion" — or the death-in-life and consequent regeneration which are the hope for earth. Dickens' final hope is in the possibility of some kind of regeneration, and in man's mortality itself, and in the kind of tenacious perpetuation this mortality implies, and in the inevitable return to reality after social posture and unreality it requires. For behind all the social themes is a strong sense of the unreality of that part of man's life he creates for himself on earth. Death and misery are the realities against which this unreality can be assessed. Symbol of death and reality is the tidal river, which Swinburne called the real protagonist of *Our Mutual Friend*; and indicative too of the continuity behind man's mortality — the constant river that subsists in the tides — is the way the living verge into death and return in this novel, or the way the dead reach back to affect the living, or the way the living live on the dead and on the river. The river symbol is not new for Dickens, but it has ramifications here that make it a more cogent and bearing symbol for him than it has ever been before.

The novel commences on the river, with Gaffer Hexam, rowed by his daughter, fishing for the dead bodies he rifles for a living. When Lizzie shows revulsion for what he is doing, Gaffer turns on her and says, of the river:

> "As if it wasn't your living! As if it wasn't meat and drink to you! . . .
> "How can you be so thankless to your best friend, Lizzie? The very fire that warmed you when you were a baby, was picked out of the river alongside the coal barges. The very basket that you slept in, the tide washed ashore. The very rockers that I put it upon to make a cradle of it, I cut out of a piece of wood that drifted from some ship or another."

So, at the very outset of the novel, the terms of the flux between life and death are suggested, and the river is seen as a generative power. A moment later, talking to Riderhood, Hexam defends his distinction between robbing the living and robbing the dead:

> "Has a dead man any use for money? It is possible for a dead man to have money? What world does a dead man belong to? T'other world. What world does money belong to? This world. How can money be a corpse's? Can a corpse own it, want it, spend it, claim it, miss it?"

A connection is made between the social themes of the novel, in which money is central, and those other themes which are the context in which the social themes attain their fullest meaning. The same is true in the next chap-

ter, when the tyrannical conditions of old Harmon's will
are related to Hexam's question: "What world does money
belong to?"

When Eugene and Mortimer go with young Hexam
to view the recovered body, they arrive where the "accumulated scum of humanity seemed to be washed from
higher grounds, like so much moral sewage, and to be
pausing until its own weight forced it over the bank
and sunk it in the river." The relation of the flow of the
river and the flow of human life is thus insisted on,
though in special, comparatively limited terms here. Earlier, the pedantic young Hexam had said that the corpse
was twice as dead as Lazarus, introducing the theme of
regeneration in a comic negative way.

At the end of the chapter, the river image is extended:

Thus, like the tides on which it had been borne to the knowledge of men, the Harmon Murder — as it came to be popularly
called — went up and down, and ebbed and flowed, now in
the town, now in the country, now among palaces, now among
hovels, now among lords and ladies and gentlefolks, now
among labourers and hammerers and ballast-heavers, until at
last, after a long interval of slack water, it got out to sea and
drifted away.

The river cuts across all inflated, unreal social distinctions in much the same way epidemic cuts across the
same boundaries in *Bleak House*, deriding these distinctions as it ignores them.

Somewhat later, Riderhood starts the false suspicion
that is to rise against the Hexams like "the tidal swell of
the river." Lizzie, thinking of this, stands looking out at
"the great black river with its dreary shores . . . soon lost

to her view in the gloom," and "unable to see into the vast blank misery of a life suspected, and fallen away from by good and bad, but knowing that it lay there dim before her, stretching away to the great ocean, Death." Here, of course, the river is used quite overtly as a symbol for the passage of life itself — in its motion, mystery, swell, and obscurity.

A curious but not really whimsical detail of the relations between dead and living is introduced by Wegg's desire to reclaim his dead leg from Venus. This is tied further to the social theme of money and is seen as part of Wegg's general acquisitiveness, and Venus, of course, is a purveyor of dead things to the living for money.

When Rokesmith asks Boffin to appoint him his secretary he says: "I have been superseded as to some slight intentions I had, and I may say that I have now to begin life." This may recall Richard Carstone's dying statement, of his "need to begin the world." But, given what has actually happened to Rokesmith, it peculiarly reinforces the retributive-regenerative function of the river in this novel.

Riderhood and Hexam are described as creatures of the slime of the river, Riderhood as a kind of water-rat, "a furry animal . . . drowned and decaying." The river punishes its own creatures for their crimes. So Hexam is drowned in the river, and dragged in by his own boat even as he has dragged in the corpses he has rifled. His recovered body soaks a shape into the ground it lies on like the bloody shape soaked into the bottom of his boat. The same power of retribution will in time reach out for Riderhood too.

After Hexam's death, his daughter devotes much of

her life to making restitution for his deeds — again the reaching out of the dead to affect the living. Riderhood defends his calumny against Hexam by asking, in an echo of Hexam's earlier defense of himself, "Can words hurt a dead man, Captain? I only ask you fair"; and Rokesmith gives the answer: "They can hurt the memory of a dead man, and they can hurt his living children."

All comes together clearly in young Harmon's dream-revery: "I came back, shrinking from my father's money, shrinking from my father's memory," he says. Central to this revery is the river, and the memories themselves flow like a river. The river is again an agent of retribution in the death of Radfoot disguised as Harmon. It is also the agent of regeneration, of the death and rebirth, for Harmon, who is thrown into the river from one bank, and emerges he knows not how on the other bank, with his old identity lost, a "living-dead man." He queries himself: "John Harmon is dead. Should John Harmon come to life?" He sometimes thinks of himself as a man who has been dead; and it is the barrier of his dead father's will that separates him from Bella Wilfer.

Riderhood gets a warning from the river, and the chance for a new life, and ignores both. While "slinking about in his boat," he is cut down by a steamer. The doctors examine him, and decide that "it is worth while trying to reanimate" him. At first, "like us all . . . when we wake — he is instinctively unwilling to be restored to the consciousness of this existence, and would be left dormant, if he could." Witnesses, and particularly his daughter, "have some vague idea that the old evil is drowned out of him, and that if he should happily come back to resume his occupation of the empty form that lies upon the bed, his spirit will be altered." This hope is foundless, however. "The low, bad, unimpressible face is coming up from the depths of the river, or what other depths, to the surface again" — and Riderhood is unchanged. Yet not entirely unchanged, for he leaves behind in the river the fur cap which had earlier signified his relation to the river, and the boat which had given him his river occupation.

Betty Higden makes the last stage of "her pilgrimage," her "toiling way along the roads of life," walking along the river, which evokes the image of miserable life running into the solace of death: "she heard the tender river whispering to many like herself, 'Come to me, come to me!' " Death in the arms of the river is "peacefuller than among the pauper wards."

Riderhood, the lock-keeper, misinterprets the river's warning, saying that having been drowned once and come back to life, he cannot be drowned again. But Lizzie uses her old knowledge gained from her father on the river to save Wrayburn, securing him to the boat much the way Gaffer secures the corpse in the first chapter of the novel. She is herself conscious of this, and thanks Heaven "for that old time," and for her chance to "turn to good at last" her old shame.

Lizzie is reconciled to the past, and the power of her dead father to injure her is finished. But there is Wrayburn too, and when Lizzie drags him into the boat, she sees his "disfigured face," so disfigured "that his mother might have covered it." What we have here is a representation of the death of Eugene's old life, and a representation too of the possibility of his regeneration. Later,

Wrayburn lies in a room with "the river outside the windows flowing on to the vast ocean." It is the basic river image once more, heightened this time by Eugene's precarious situation. He moves without will between consciousness and unconsciousness, between life and death. To the friends sitting by his bed, this shifting resembles the "frequent rising of a drowning man from the deep, to sink again . . . As the man rising from the deep would disappear the sooner for fighting with the water, so he in his desperate struggle went down again." If Wrayburn is really to return, he must be regenerated, begin the world again, have a new life. His marriage to Lizzie is his first decisive step in this direction, though he is not yet sure himself that he can live as he must live if he is to be reborn, and he thinks it may be better for him just to die. Wrayburn does, we are told, have a new life, but for Riderhood and Headstone no regeneration is possible, and they die grappling together in the river.

It is against this urgent sense of the tragedy and hope of man's mortality that the social world of *Our Mutual Friend* must be assessed. Nor is this really a special or historical judgment we are asked to make. The essential facts are really unchanged and unlikely to change.

It has been peculiar to the nature of the novel, particularly the English novel, to be extensive without being comprehensive. The longer the novel, the more likely it is to seem unfinished, to end arbitrarily. The impression is fortified when we compare the novel to the older, higher art forms with which it asks comparison, the long poem and the drama. This failing is related to the novel's strength, for its relative informality contributes to its special capacity to deal with the chaotic variousness of the modern experience. Yet some novelists have not been satisfied to accept the generic weakness for the strength it implies, and in these four novels Dickens tried with increasing success to create a vivid vision of society that would be at once extensive and comprehensive.

Perhaps at the expense of some of the ebullient, seemingly spontaneous invention of the earlier novels, he contrived to shape his teeming materials — by systematic accretion of significant detail, by purposeful plotting, and by the creation of an informing context — into a vision that, seeming to represent the world, explains the explicable, and wonders at the great residual mystery. The attempt is of the most ambitious, and the company that has managed it with anything like his degree of success is small.

Chapter Five

THE SENSE OF SELF

With no more than the first words of the novel on paper, Dickens wrote to Forster that *Great Expectations* would "be written in the first person throughout, and . . . you will find the hero to be a boy-child, like David . . . To be quite sure I had fallen into no unconscious repetitions, I read David Copperfield again the other day, and was affected by it to a degree you would hardly believe." [1] In his own mind, the two books, *David Copperfield* and *Great Expectations*, were a pair. Comparison reveals not only a number of precise parallels, large and small, between the two books, but much too about the change in perspective that makes the two books so different despite these parallels.

David Copperfield was written in 1849–50, *Great Expectations* in 1860–61. The crucial years for the hardening or darkening of Dickens' thinking are the middle fifties. The two autobiographical novels span this time almost symmetrically, and the difference in perspective and tone accurately represents the change in Dickens' view of himself in his world. *Great Expectations* is in a sense the mirror image of *Copperfield*.

The earlier and more explicitly autobiographical novel

[1] *Letters* III, 186, October 1860.

is a success story, its dominant mood pathetic. *Great Ex-pectations* describes a movement away from success, and its dominant mood is ironic. When the materials of the two novels are most similar, the change in point of view is often clearest. For example, Australia, which is a Utopia for Mr. Peggotty and the Micawbers, is a place of hard exile for Magwitch. Betsy Trotwood is made eccentric but wise by her disappointments in love, but Miss Havi-sham is crazed by hers. In *David Copperfield*, the moral view of crime is simple, uncomplicated; in *Great Expec-tations*, the more realistic and complicated view of crime provides much of the richness of the book. The depravity of Steerforth is mitigated; that of Bentley Drummle is undisguised and is given purposeful social context. The incompetence of David's mother is treated affectionately, but Mrs. Pocket is vicious.

In other cases, however, the parallelism in material in-dicates little of the difference in quality of the books. Herbert is a foil for Pip much as Traddles is for David. Biddy is the Agnes of the later book. The wedding of Wemmick and Miss Skiffins is clearly reminiscent of the wedding of Barkis and Peggotty. Similarly, the scar-ring of Estella's mother recalls the scarring of Rosa Dartle. Pip's servant is much like David's page; the butcher boy becomes Trabb's boy. Pumblechook's exam-ination of Pip in arithmetic recalls a similar examination of David by Mr. Murdstone.

The number of these parallels (and there are more), both simple and complicated, major and minor, shows how often the two novels are embarked on related pieces of fictional exploration. It affords, too, specific and de-tailed evidence of the change in Dickens' view between the time of *David Copperfield* and that of *Great Expectations*. Yet the continuity of his imagination, of which the comparison provides at least equal evidence, is more profound than the change in his view or construction of those facts and configurations of experience in which his imagination is founded.

DAVID COPPERFIELD

David Copperfield is a novel about worldly prudence; and conversely, about the dangers of imprudence and trust. Nearly every character in the novel, nearly every event of importance, nearly every relationship can be regarded as an example or variation on the theme of prudence: in business, in money matters, in friendship, in love. This consideration precedes David's birth. Miss Trotwood talks of the unworldliness of her dead nephew, David's father, who "Calls a house a rookery when there's not a rook near it, and takes the birds on trust, because he sees the nests!" Miss Trotwood is full of compassionate contempt for her nephew's "trust," but she has herself been the victim of trust in love, and is to be a victim of financial trust also. David's father had shown his imprudence in other and graver ways too. He had married a child wife, a form of imprudence that is to be part of his son's inheritance; and though when he dies he leaves his wife with an adequate income, a fact that surprises Miss Trotwood, he leaves her, as she herself confesses, totally unprepared for "being quite alone and dependent on myself in this rough world." The money he has left her in fact only undoes her, bringing the Murdstones to prey on her.

The beginning of the novel suggests a shape for what is to come. Even David's minor misadventures as a boy are likely to be misadventures of imprudence or unfounded trust: with the waiter at the inn, for example, who eats his dinner, or the carter who runs away with his box. This is a story in which innocence may and does have ultimate rewards, but is first much abused and preyed on. Mr. Mell is betrayed by David, bullied by Steerforth, abused by Creakle. Tommy Traddles, too, is abused for his feeling heart and good nature — by Steerforth, by Creakle, by Micawber. It is Traddles' trusting unworldliness, not any particular failure of either industry or intelligence, that makes him the foil to that part of Copperfield's history that is an account of the way to fame and worldly success. Dr. Strong is a trusting innocent too, who is preyed on by his wife's relatives, and is saved from actual cuckoldry, though not from the onus of it, by little more than Dickens' inclination to respect propriety. Dora Spenlow and Clara Copperfield represent a kind of extreme of innocence and trust, and each of them, in the scheme of this world, has to die young.

Dickens' inclination to respect propriety is only this, not a rule, even as Victorian propriety itself is more a convention of public admission than a description of conduct. Sex has its place and force in this novel, even though it is treated guardedly, and is seen equally in terms of prudence and trust — trust in this case being the trust in passion itself, which leads to ruin. In addition to the unfortunate loves of David's father, and Clara Copperfield, and Betsy Trotwood — all examples of imprudent love and its ravages — there are other examples in which the sexual passion is more openly at issue: Emily's seduction by Steerforth; the psychotic passion of Rosa Dartle for Steerforth; the ruin of Emily's friend, Martha; Murdstone's insane second wife; and Mrs. Strong's infatuation with her no-good cousin, Jack Maldon. In the last case, the infatuation itself has far more force than does its comfortable resolution.

Imprudence in love brings disaster; and prudence — sensible love, aware of advantage — brings happiness. Tommy Traddles, though he waits many years to earn his marriage, is at last blissfully happy, and Barkis, who marries Peggotty for her cooking and housewifery, is domestically blessed too. Barkis's caution in love is related to his caution with money. Both are funny, even a little pathetic, but both turn out well.

The history of David's loves is a history of the mistakes survived in the learning of prudence. His first love, for Emily, is an idyllic child's love, but without future. Miss Shepherd, "a boarder at the Misses Nettingall's establishment," is a less poetic version of the same kind of love. "The eldest Miss Larkins," who dances with officers, is the Victorian English equivalent for the convention of the young man's older first mistress. Dora Spenlow, who signifies David's congenital imprudence in matters of love, is a self-confessed child-wife, unable even to manage her account books or order her house. Her attractiveness is rather pre-sexual, and like Clara she is unfit for adult life, and must die. Finally, of course, David prudently marries Agnes Wickfield and lives happily ever after.

While other characters are more or less permanently committed to their early choices or accidents, David has

a succession of chances and choices. Other people are vulnerable, and their humanity lies in good part in their
vulnerability, but David becomes increasingly an invul-
nerable figure, destined for success no matter what happens to him. Though the child David exists as a seen and
felt presence in the novel, the older David becomes more
and more a seeing eye and recounting voice to whom
things do not happen in the same way that they happen
to other people, and who tends therefore to recede. This
effect is anticipated in the very first sentence of the novel:
"Whether I shall turn out to be the hero of my own life,
or whether that station will be held by anybody else,
these pages must show."

In part, this recession of the central character from
the novel — a recession in intensity, if not in importance
— can be attributed to the technique of narration employed. The story is told in the first person, from the
vantage of the adult David. He can see himself as a boy
with some detachment, in the round. When the narrator
approaches closer to the time of the telling of the story,
however, he can no longer separate himself sufficiently
from the hero whose adventures he recounts. But the
strategy of the novel, too, affects this progressive paling
of David in the story. *David Copperfield* is really a rags-
to-riches story, or, with more convolutions, a series of
descents and ascents heading toward a final ascent. As
early as the time of his employment at Murdstone and
Grinby's, David says: "I knew from the first, that if I
could not do my work as well as any of the rest, I could
not hold myself above slight and contempt." Now
though success may capture our interest because of its
reference to our own aspirations, it is unlikely to capture

our imagination. The real resources of literary art are rather on the side of failure.

But if all this is so, it still remains that *David Copperfield* has captured the imagination of readers for a century. Dickens himself spoke of it as his "favourite child" among all his books, and specifically of how the book grasped his imagination: "It would concern the reader little, perhaps, to know how sorrowfully the pen is laid down at the close of a two-years' imaginative task; or how an Author feels as if he were dismissing some portion of himself into the shadowy world, when a crowd of the creatures of his brain are going from him for ever . . . no one can ever believe this Narrative in the reading more than I believed it in the writing."

This statement in a late preface reflects and even duplicates part of an extraordinary letter Dickens wrote to Forster as he was finishing the writing of *David Copperfield:* "I am within three pages of the shore; and am strangely divided, as usual in such cases, between sorrow and joy. Oh, my dear Forster, if I were to say half of what *Copperfield* makes me feel to-night, how strangely, even to you, I should be turned inside out! I seem to be sending some part of myself into the Shadowy World."

That there is a power, as suggested, in this novel, few readers will contest. That this power is not directly related to the overt moral of the novel means quite simply that Dickens is still, in 1849–50, endeavoring to deny the tragic implications of life that he, in fact, sees with great clarity and responds to with greatest imaginative force. On the surface, *David Copperfield* asserts the need for prudence and the beauty of success. But the power of the novel comes from its vital rendering of the beauty of incaution and the poignancy of limitation and defeat. In its plot, *David Copperfield* is conventionally Victorian. But essentially and imaginatively, it subverts its own contentions.

The novel is autobiographical to varying extents in its different parts, but most when it recounts the dark London period of David's childhood. It is this period that informs all the rest of David's life, and of the novel, even when it is past:

A remoteness had come upon the old Blunderstone life — which seemed to lie in the haze of an immeasurable distance; and . . . a curtain had for ever fallen on my life at Murdstone and Grinby's. No one has ever raised that curtain since. I have lifted it for a moment, even in this narrative, with a reluctant hand, and dropped it gladly. The remembrance of that life is fraught with so much pain to me, with so much mental suffering and want of hope, that I have never had the courage even to examine how long I was doomed to lead it. Whether it lasted for a year, or more, or less, I do not know. I only know that it was, and ceased to be; and that I have written, and there I leave it.

In the fragment of an autobiography that Dickens showed to Forster, there follows after the blacking factory account a strikingly similar passage, ending: "I have never, until I now impart it to this paper, in any burst of confidence with any one, my own wife not excepted, raised the curtain I then dropped, thank God." David shares with Dickens not only certain grim experiences of childhood, but also the will and inability to forget them.

Though the scheme of *David Copperfield* points to the desirability of social status, the sanctity and authority

of status are often under attack. David's first distinction,
or assertion of self, is an abortive revolt against authority,
the biting of Mr. Murdstone's hand. He has come to re-
cite his lessons for his mother, with the two Murdstones
as audience. Mr. Murdstone, in the process of bending a
"lithe and limber" cane when David comes in, warns the
boy that he must do better this time with his lessons.
Given this encouragement, David of course forgets
everything. When he has failed completely, Murdstone
leads him from the room to his own room and beats him
cruelly. David first begs him to stop, then catches his
hand in his teeth and bites "it through. It sets my teeth
on edge to think of it." Murdstone then beats him "as if
he would have beaten me to death," and locks him in
his room alone, feverish and raging.

How well I remember, when my smart and passion began to
cool, how wicked I began to feel!

I sat listening for a long while, but there was not a sound.
I crawled up from the floor, and saw my face in the glass, so
swollen, red, and ugly that it almost frightened me. My stripes
were sore and stiff, and made me cry afresh, when I moved;
but they were nothing to the guilt I felt. It lay heavier on my
breast than if I had been a most atrocious criminal, I dare say.

More striking here than the cruelty and sadism of
Murdstone's authority is the fact that David is corrupted
by that authority. Though the reader rejoices in the
biting of Murdstone's hand, David himself is appalled by
what he has done, his guilt lies heavier on him than his
pain, and he feels "a most atrocious criminal." George Orwell, a careful reader of Dickens, tells a similar story of
his own boyhood: of how, beaten by the master of his

school for bedwetting, he felt guilty not only for his
weak bladder, but also for the loss of the master's cane,
broken over his back in the course of the beating. The
attack in *David Copperfield* on the sadism of authority
continues with Creakle and Tungay, at David's first
school, whose chief victim is Traddles, the best-hearted
boy in the school, and who fear and fail to exercise any
authority over Steerforth, who genuinely needs it.

There is subversive humor too in *David Copperfield*,
at the expense of institutions and honored professions.
The intrusive Chapter 61 is the most blatant example, in
which Creakle's educational genius has finally been properly put to work managing a model prison, among whose
prisoners the shining stars of conduct and piety are Uriah
Heep and Littimer. The legal profession too, not re-
served for derision in *Bleak House* alone, comes in for
the usual treatment. Mr. Spenlow tells David of the "very
pretty pickings" likely to come from a disputed will for
a "neat little estate of thirty or forty thousand pounds";
but he denies the possibility that there could be a better
way of handling such matters. After all, he argues,
"when the price of wheat per bushel had been highest,
the Commons had been busiest." Finally, David's occupation as a Parliamentary reporter provides full opportunity to disparage the House of Commons more directly.

The humor of British institutions is bitter humor, re-
lating as it does to the dire life of the lower class, of
which however, there are really only brief glimpses in
David Copperfield once David himself leaves the blacking factory: Mr. Mell's visit to his mother, for instance,
or the view of the house and quarter in which the fallen

girl Martha lives in London. The Micawbers' life provides a similar insight, though refracted by the dispropor-
tioning views of Mr. and Mrs. Micawber; and even Uriah
Heep and his mother are seen as, in some part, victims
of poverty and the British system of providing for the
poor in a degrading way that fosters hypocrisy.

Dickens' darker vision, though, is founded on more
than the existence of bad character and bad institutions.
In an unforgettable passage, David thinks of his mother,
after her death, as the younger, unworn mother of his
infancy, and of himself as the dead and untried baby
buried with her, "hushed forever on her bosom." The
sense of aging, of death, and of loss — the passage of
the river of life into the sea — pervades the book and
gives it weight: David's loss of Dora, and of a vision of
the thoughtless beauty of youth; the loss of Steerforth to
David, to Rosa Dartle, to Mrs. Steerforth, and the agony
that comes to each when death spells the end of the
possibility of reconciliation; the death of Dora's dog at
the instant of his mistress's death; Martha's attempt to
drown herself in the river, and the deaths of Ham and
Steerforth in the sea, in which always the river of life
loses its identity; Barkis's departure with the tide. Against
all this, Steerforth's picture of life as a race to be won
is a preposterous affront; and, indeed, any notion of success is an affront, given the pathetic insufficiency of prudence or wisdom to slow or change the current of man's
life into death.

GREAT EXPECTATIONS

The end of the first part of *Great Expectations* suggests a context for the entire novel:

I walked away at a good pace, thinking it was easier to go than I had supposed it would be, and reflecting that it would never have done to have an old shoe thrown after the coach, in sight of all the High-Street. I whistled and made nothing of going. But the village was very peaceful and quiet, and the light mists were solemnly rising, as if to show me the world, and I had been so innocent and little there, and all beyond was so unknown and great, that in a moment with a strong heave and sob I broke into tears. . . .

So subdued I was by those tears, and by their breaking out again in the course of the quiet walk, that when I was on the coach, and it was clear of the town, I deliberated with an aching heart whether I would not get down when we changed horses and walk back, and have another evening at home, and a better parting. We changed, and I had not made up my mind, and still reflected for my comfort that it would be quite practicable to get down and walk back, when we changed again. . . .

We changed again, and yet again, and it was now too late and too far to go back, and I went on. And the mists had all solemnly risen now, and the world lay spread before me.

No over-subtlety is required at this point to remember the departure of Adam and Eve from Eden — behind them the cherubim on the ground looking, Milton tells us, like mist risen from the marshes, while the other way, "The World was all before them."

The usefulness of this suggestion depends on caution. The suggestion is slight, and *Great Expectations* is no formal allegory. It would not have occurred to Dickens that one book could or should stand upon another. Obviously, however, the departure from Eden belongs in no exclusive way to Milton, but has become one of those great general metaphors by which man explains his rea-

sonably inexplicable condition. The slight verbal parallel
between the end of the first part of *Great Expectations*
and the end of *Paradise Lost* may only be happy chance,
but it exercises an imaginative control nonetheless over
this perhaps most controlled of Dickens' novels.

The Eden from which young Philip Pirrip departs
does not conform much to our idea of the garden: the
marshes extending from the river where the prison ships
are perpetually anchored; the warning gibbet on the
shore; the mists and fogs and damp, cold weather; the
unpromising village with its merchant rulers of the High-
Street, its rough inn and pub, its tight provincial society;
and the uncomfortable house by the forge where Mrs.
Gargery brings up not only her young brother, but her
husband too, "by hand." None of this is much to the point
except that it has the quality of being a place apart,
isolated largely, though not completely, from the world.

What figures most here is not the cosmography of
place, but the innocence of Pip's soul and mind in this
place, an innocence which leads him to infer the characters
and appearances of his parents and brothers from their
tombstones; to love Joe "because the dear fellow let me
love him"; to pity the desolation of the escaped convict and
be glad that he enjoys his stolen food; to believe that the
exhortation of his catechism, "to walk in the same all the
days of my life," binds him to take the same route without variation whenever he leaves his house to walk through
the village. This innocence, too, enables him to discrimi-
nate justly between good and bad, and wisely among
people as to those who are his friends and those who are
not. Pip's innocence is fractured by expectation —
planted by his sister and Pumblechook, encouraged by

the secret plans of Magwitch and of Miss Havisham.
The objects of his expectation are, conventionally
enough, property and love, scarcely distinguishable in
his thinking, but each considered in detailed variation in
this novel.

The evil of property lies in its tendency to use its
possessors instead of being used by them. The point is
made unambiguously and with force. Pip's first genuine
act in *Great Expectations*, and an act from which ensue
the consequences that in good part make the novel, is to
steal food and a file from his home for the starving escaped convict Magwitch. It is notable that the guilt that
haunts his mind has nothing to do with the genuinely
serious matter of aiding an escaped and dangerous convict. It is his own theft he worries about, and not so
much the stolen file as the stolen food, the broken vittles.
Joe Gargery, who remains in the Eden of innocence
throughout the novel, and is the control or fixed point
in relation to which Pip's wandering is measured, makes
overt the moral significance of this theft, when the escaped convict, to protect Pip, says that it was he who
stole the food from the Gargerys' house: " 'God knows
you're welcome to it — so far as it was ever mine,' returned Joe, with a saving remembrance of Mrs. Joe. 'We
don't know what you have done, but we wouldn't have
you starved to death for it, poor miserable fellow creature — Would us, Pip?' "

Joe tries to bolster Pip in his innocence, but Mrs. Joe
is another matter. For her, property is sacred and uncomfortable, like some people's religion. Her prepara-
tions for Christmas dinner blight the holiday, and when
she walks to town, she carries "a basket like the Great

Seal of England in plaited straw, a pair of pattens, a
spare shawl, and an umbrella, though it was a fine bright
day." Pip was not clear whether "these articles were carried penitentially or ostentatiously," but he thought they
were probably "displayed as articles of property — much
as Cleopatra or any other soverign lady on the Rampage
might exhibit her wealth in a pageant or procession."

Pumblechook (a good example of Dickens' genius for
fitting names) is far worse than Mrs. Gargery, and it is
he who pushes Pip into the Havisham connection, bullies
and maltreats him, flatters him when his fortunes are risen,
and turns on him self-righteously and full of injury when
they fall. But the real nightmare of property is provided
by Miss Havisham in Satis House. A rough irony of
names is used frequently in *Great Expectations,* starting
with the title itself; of the name of the Havisham house,
Estella says: "It meant when it was given, that whoever
had this house, could want nothing else. They must have
been easily satisfied in those days, I should think." In a
ruin of old symbolic goods, Miss Havisham lives a living
death, and plots her vicarious vengeance on victims who
have only a token culpability for her tragedy. It is her
goods, her wealth, that have ruined her in the first place
by attracting Compeyson to her, and now she will have
the goods work in reverse, by making Estella rich, im-
pregnable, heart-breaking.

To Pip at first she seems, quite accurately, a waxwork
or a skeleton amidst her goods, but this perception does
not save him from becoming a victim to his expectations
of property, and of property as a means of access to love.
Miss Havisham encourages his delusion that she is his pa-
troness, the cause and source of his expectations, and

that, as she intends him to have fortune, she intends him to have Estella too, and to be prepared for her and made more worthy of her by this money. So he is least prepared for the ultimate revelation of the true source of his expectations. In fact, he thinks his bond of complicity with Magwitch to be reduced, almost written off by his fortune:

If I had often thought before, with something allied to shame, of my companionship with the fugitive whom I had once seen limping among those graves, what were my thoughts on this Sunday, when the place recalled the wretch, ragged and shivering, with his felon iron and badge! My comfort was, that it happened a long time ago, and that he had doubtless been transported a long way off, and that he was dead to me, and might be veritably dead into the bargain.

No more low wet grounds, no more dykes and sluices, no more of these grazing cattle — though they seemed, in their dull manner, to wear a more respectful air now, and to face round, in order that they might stare as long as possible at the possessor of such great expectations — farewell, monotonous acquaintances of my childhood, henceforth I was for London and greatness: not for smith's work in general and for you! I made my exultant way to the old Battery, and, lying down there to consider the question whether Miss Havisham intended me for Estella, fell asleep.

But it is the fortune that makes Pip's bond to Magwitch indissoluble. In the world of this novel, property is harmless only when it is allowed no false aura of dignity or pretense, when it is clearly useful, and bears clear and preferably comic marks of human contrivance and effort. Of such property Wemmick's little estate at Walworth is the chief example; and in this setting there is a happy, loving society.

Of Pip's second expectation, love, Dickens draws an
equally forbidding and infrequently relieved picture. It
is useful to remember Dickens' own life at this point,
though not to elaborate on it tenuously. By 1860, his marriage had ended in a legal separation, but was still a
source of unrest and bitterness to him; and his relationship with Ellen Ternan too, now well past its first
flush, had settled into some sort of disappointing resolution of its own. At least two critics [2] have found verbal
plays and echoings of Ellen Ternan's name in the names
of a number of Dickens' late heroines, including the Estella of *Great Expectations*. These heroines reflect too,
they think, Ellen Ternan's failing in her relationship with
Dickens: coldness, frigidity. Be this as it may — and the
evidence gives the speculation great weight — it is clear
enough that Estella is as cold and distant, as removed, as
the stars her name suggests. She warns Pip herself that
she has "no heart"; and, unable to manage a normal response to love, she has the decency to reserve herself
from anyone capable of better, and gives herself instead
to Bentley Drummle, who is as unfeeling as she, but a
sensual brute in addition.

In some really frightful way here, anything like normal
sexuality always makes for terror and tragedy. Miss
Havisham falls passionately in love with Compeyson
and is victimized by her love. The love of Magwitch and
his wife ends in violence. Orlick, who desires Biddy,
kills Mrs. Gargery and tries to kill Pip too. Mr. Pocket
is victimized by his early love for Mrs. Pocket, and Joe
by his for Pip's sister. The only relationships between

[2] Edmund Wilson; and Ada Nisbet in *Dickens and Ellen Ternan*
(Berkeley, California, 1952).

men and women that work out are reasonable, nonpassionate relationships: the middle-aged love of Wemmick and Miss Skiffins; Joe's fatherly love for Biddy, and her motherly love for him; the patient domestic attachment of Herbert and Clara; and the final rapprochement of Pip and Estella after their misspent youths are well behind them.

It is no wonder, then, that with his great expectations of property and love, Pip comes a cropper. There is no doubt that these bad expectations seem to make inevitable his disappointments. Yet again, here as in *David Copperfield*, fate is beyond good or bad choice, beyond prudence or prodigality. Pip's profoundest fate works by indirection, in which good comes out of bad and bad out of good. The basic first action in the novel is the encounter with Magwitch in the cemetery. Out of a mixture of fear and compassion, Pip helps the escaped convict, bringing him food, and a file with which to remove his fetters. Initially, everything seems to condone Pip's actions as simple charity toward someone in distress.

But the situation is not this simple. Magwitch is an escaped convict, a man both capable and guilty of great violence. After his escapade, Pip is in fear of the police, and feels guilty for his failure of openness with Joe. But these are comparatively minor matters, only the direct consequences of his complicity with Magwitch. The indirect consequences are more dire. When his sister is struck over the head with a heavy object, that object turns out to be "a convict's leg-iron . . . filed asunder." Pip is certain it is Magwitch's iron, filed off with the file with which he provided him. Still Pip temporizes and does not disclose what he knows to Joe. He contains it,

even as he kept his council when the strange man in the
pub stirred a drink with a file, and presented him with a
shilling wrapped in two one-pound notes, and when he
had bad dreams at night, and thought — rather insuffi-
ciently to the point — what a "guiltily coarse and common thing it was, to be on secret terms of conspiracy
with convicts."

The richest morality and realism of *Great Expectations* depends on the figure of Magwitch. The convict is
a dangerous, violent man, and unregenerate in his violence, as his final murder of Compeyson shows. His
wife, Molly, too, with her strong scarred wrists, is a
woman whose violence is kept down only by strong
restraint, her own and Jaggers'. Yet the violence of these
two (and of many others, it is suggested) is not spontaneous, or not always and entirely so. In part at least, they
are the victims of poverty and of a class system that
fosters and gives protection to weak or evil villains like
Miss Havisham's brother or Compeyson. Official justice,
the justice of the courts and prisons, is an unfeeling and
corrupt justice whose drunken ministers sell good seats in
court for half-a-crown, and buy second-hand clothes
cheap from the executioner.

The nature of this justice is made clear in the account
of Magwitch's trial:

The trial was very short and very clear. Such things as
could be said for him, were said — how he had taken to industrious habits, and had thriven lawfully and reputably. But,
nothing could unsay the fact that he had returned, and was
there in the presence of the Judge and Jury. It was impossible
to try him for that, and do otherwise than find him guilty.

At that time it was the custom (as I learnt from my terrible

experience of that Sessions) to devote a concluding day to
the passing of Sentences, and to make a finishing effect with
the Sentence of Death. But for the indelible picture that my
remembrance now holds before me, I could scarcely believe,
even as I write these words, that I saw two-and-thirty men
and women put before the Judge to receive that sentence together. Foremost among the two-and-thirty was he; seated,
that he might get breath enough to keep life in him.

The whole scene starts out again in the vivid colours of the
moment, down to the drops of April rain on the windows of
the court, glittering in the rays of April sun. Penned in the
dock, as I again stood outside it at the corner with his hand
in mine, were the two-and-thirty men and women; some defi-
ant, some stricken with terror, some sobbing and weeping,
some covering their faces, some staring gloomily about.
There had been shrieks from among the women convicts, but
they had been stilled, and a hush had succeeded. The sheriffs
with their great chains and nosegays, other civic gewgaws and
monsters, criers, ushers, a great gallery full of people — a
large theatrical audience — looked on, as the two-and-thirty
and the Judge were solemnly confronted. Then, the Judge
addressed them. Among the wretched creatures before him
whom he must single out for special address, was one who
almost from infancy had been an offender against the laws. . . .

The sun was striking in at the great windows of the court,
through the glittering drops of rain upon the glass, and it
made a broad shaft of light between the two-and-thirty and
the Judge, linking both together, and perhaps reminding
some among the audience, how both were passing on, with
absolute equality, to the greater Judgment that knoweth all
things and cannot err. Rising for a moment, a distinct speck
of face in this way of light, the prisoner said, "My Lord, I
have received my sentence of Death from the Almighty, but
I bow to yours," and sat down again. There was some hushing,
and the Judge went on with what he had to say to the rest.

Then, they were all formally doomed, and some of them were supported out, and some of them sauntered out with a haggard look of bravery, and a few nodded to the gallery, and two or three shook hands, and others went out chewing the fragments of herb they had taken from the sweet herbs lying about. He went last of all, because of having to be helped from his chair and to go very slowly; and he held my hand while all the others were removed, and while the audience got up (putting their dresses right, as they might at church or elsewhere) and pointed down at this criminal or that, and most of all at him and me.

In contrast to this justice of mass reprisal and of brutalizing public spectacle, Magwitch's administration of a personal justice that rewards good and punishes evil and takes the consequences for its own acts has its splendor and dignity, even though it cannot be allowed.

Pip, after visiting Newgate with Wemmick, thinks how strange it is that the taint of prison and crime should pervade his fortune and advancement. He thinks, too, what a contrast all this is to "the beautiful young Estella." But what he must still learn, of course, is that Estella is in fact the daughter of Magwitch and Molly. Eventually, he not only knows but is also reconciled. He comes not only to be unashamed of the dying Magwitch, but genuinely to love him, and just before Magwitch dies, Pip is able to tell him that his daughter whom he thought dead is alive, that she is a lady and very beautiful, and that he loves her. As Miss Havisham's foster-daughter and her false heir, Estella and Pip cannot come together. As Magwitch's true daughter and his deprived heir, they will.

There are no triumphantly happy endings in Dickens' later novels. Instead, there is the second chance that comes after chastening and acceptance. In *David Cop-perfield* still, the happiness that comes after chastening seems almost able to disregard its own past — it is a virtually uninjured, full happiness. But in the later books, life is made more consequential, and people are what they are because of what they have been. Their happiness is a reconciliation to knowledge, and in these later books too, knowledge without reconciliation produces the riven mind, as in the case of Flora Finching. The alternatives Dickens offers, with increasing exclusiveness, are either madness, or the muted happiness that comes after acceptance.

The actual reconciliation of Pip and Estella at the end of *Great Expectations* was, as everyone knows, not in the original draft of the novel, but was added when Bul-wer-Lytton objected to the unrelievedly somber tone of the original ending. But the limited optimism of the resolution of the novel does not depend on, and is not modified by, the changed ending. Pip has lost all his property, and has only such money as he earns by his own labors. Estella too has lost all her property. The Estella whom Pip had loved, and expected, really exists no longer, nor has he won the relatively romantic consolation of Biddy. And he is reconciled to his losses. Both he and Estella, we are told, have paled but grown better with age.

So after many years they meet again on a misty early evening on the grounds of Miss Havisham's old house — in the ruined garden, in fact, to return to the metaphor of the loss of Eden. Now Estella has a heart, and can confess to Pip's place in it. She, of course, has her place still in his heart, too. It is reasonable then to suggest that Pip has reentered the ruined Eden in order to leave again, as Adam had left, chastened and with his chastened Eve: "I took her hand in mine, and we went out of the ruined place; and, as the morning mists had risen long ago when I first left the forge, so, the evening mists were rising now, and in all the broad expanse of tranquil light they showed to me, I saw no shadow of another parting from her."

Great Expectations provides a correction to the conventional optimism of *David Copperfield*. Pip must learn that fortune is not the way to happiness. Perhaps, too, Dickens is celebrating the losses that accompanied his success and the consequences of his will to forget his past. Certainly, to the modern reader, *Great Expectations* seems the more adult book — in its view of love, of success, of society; and its tighter structure and allegorical overtones are likely to please the chaste and intellectual modern taste more than the loose structure and folk tale elements of *David Copperfield*.

Yet though opinions and views may change, the basic vision of the individual imagination is relatively constant, and the greater the work of art, the more it founds the changing appearances dictated in part by view and opinion on the obsessional configurations of the imagination. Both *David Copperfield* and *Great Expectations* bear the profound marks of Dickens' imagination, and despite the many important ways in which one denies the other, essentially they reveal the same vision of life. Each of these books — *David Copperfield* as well as *Great Expectations* — is subversive, and the power of each depends on a response to the rendering of loss, of the beauty of hazard, of the horror of social injustice, and of the preposterous comedy of hypocrisy and self-delusion.

Chapter Six

ADDENDA: THE SPORTS OF PLENTY

Hard Times, A Tale of Two Cities, and *The Mystery of Edwin Drood* distinguish themselves from the main body of Dickens' mature fiction for accidental as well as considered reasons, and the three books are in turn very dissimilar. They are strongly marked in common, however, by a relative thinness of texture. In these novels, fewer minor characters and fewer sub-plots enrich the world in which the major characters act; and the world itself is rendered with less detail and fewer circumstances. There is less comedy also, and not so many of those only seemingly gratuitous events and people that lend a special authority to Dickens' created world.

In *The Mystery of Edwin Drood,* the difference seems largely intentional. Dickens apparently wished at the end to write more about individuals and less about society. Certainly *The Mystery of Edwin Drood,* though a story of individuals, maintains Dickens' consistent social concerns,[1] and John Jasper is only the last in a series of criminal types, begun already in the *Sketches* and *The Pickwick Papers* but most clearly emergent in *Oliver*

[1] As Edmund Wilson, among others, has been at pains to demonstrate.

Twist, who, though recognized for what they are, criminals, also convey a peculiarly incisive condemnation of social morals and social injustice. Nonetheless, a comparison of Jasper with Bradley Headstone — to whom he is closest not only chronologically among Dickens' criminal characters but also in temperament and situation — is an accurate measure of the reduced place of social consideration in Dickens' last novel. Yet because *The Mystery of Edwin Drood* is unfinished, it offers rather too much of a grab bag for speculation.

It is possible to speak about *Hard Times* and *A Tale of Two Cities* with a good deal more certainty. Each was written for weekly serialization [2] and each is roughly half the length of a novel written in monthly parts.[3] This is of the first importance, for Dickens' eloquent testimony to his sense of limitation and constraint in the shorter form cannot be overemphasized. During an early stage of the writing of *Hard Times*, he told Forster that "the difficulty of the space is CRUSHING" for anyone who has "had an experience of patient fiction-writing with some elbow-room always, and open places in perspective." [4] And ten years later, commencing *Our Mutual Friend*, he wrote to Wilkie Collins of being "dazed in getting back to the large canvas and the big brushes" [5] after *Great Expectations* and *A Tale of Two Cities*.

Dickens' sense of the limitations of the shorter form is

[2] *Hard Times* appeared in *Household Words*, *A Tale of Two Cities* in *All the Year Round*.
[3] *The Mystery of Edwin Drood*, planned for twelve monthly parts rather than the usual twenty, would have been close in length to one of the novels in weekly parts, but the parts themselves were the usual length for a novel in monthly parts.
[4] *Letters* II, 543, to Forster, February 1854.
[5] *Letters* III, 378, to Collins, 24 January 1864.

seen too in the purposeful way he sets his subject — the attack on the Benthamites in *Hard Times*, the admonitory analogy between England and France in *A Tale of Two Cities*. Both these novels suffer from an excessive purposefulness, which may simply be another way of saying that the world they create is deficient in density. It may be to the point also that Dickens' indeterminate debt, or sense of affinity at least, to Carlyle is more evident in these two books than anywhere else.[6] *Hard Times* is dedicated to Carlyle, and *The French Revolution* is the chief source for the revolutionary scenes in *A Tale of Two Cities*. Nor is the affinity merely superficial. *Hard Times* goes beyond a simple attack on the Benthamites to an assertion of the limits of any rational systematizing, and finally of rationalism itself; and *A Tale of Two Cities* is very nearly as anti-democratic as Carlyle could have wished it to be. Yet only in these cramped shorter novels does Dickens take so decided a position on complicated, ambiguous, and undecided questions. *Great Expectations*, the last of the shorter novels, is the only one in which the limitation in length seems to produce concision without loss of richness and vital complication.

The short form, then, sets *Hard Times* and *A Tale of Two Cities* somewhat apart from the main body of Dickens' mature fiction. *The Mystery of Edwin Drood* is similarly set off by a combination of apparent authorial intention and the accident of its incompletion. Yet of course all these novels are products of Dickens' tenaci-

---

[6] Although the constant contrast between external appearances and inner reality in *Little Dorrit* is not unrelated to the transcendentalism of *Sartor Resartus*.

ously consistent if also varied and unrepetitive genius,
and by their very differences, therefore, they tend to
make more apparent the essential characteristics of that
genius.

HARD TIMES

The recent marked increase in the reputation of *Hard
Times* has come at the expense of Dickens' general reputation. Satisfaction with this one sport of his genius has
been used as a basis on which to denigrate that genius
in its more characteristic manifestations.[7] *Hard Times*
satisfies the modern taste (in the arts alone) for economy
— in fiction, for spare writing and clearly demonstrable
form. Dickens was capable of both, but they were not
natural or congenial to him, and he chose to employ them
only under the duress of limited space. Curiously
enough, *Hard Times* grants a scant measure of the very
quality for which it argues, imaginative pleasure. Its
seriousness is so scrupulous, plain, and insistent that the
reader moves along with simple, too rarely surprised
consent, and it is worth noting that at one point Dickens
considered calling the novel "Black and White."

Yet it is silly to prolong the arbitrary see-saw between
Hard Times and the rest of Dickens' work. It is more to
the point to see that the greatest virtues of *Hard Times*
are Dickens' characteristic virtues, but less richly present in this book than in many others.

Hard Times is least interesting as an exploitation of
its avowed subject, the inadequacy of the Benthamite cal-

---

[7] Most notably by F. R. Leavis, who, in *The Great Tradition* (London, 1948), finds that *Hard Times* "has a kind of perfection as a work
of art that we don't associate with Dickens — a perfection that is one
with the sustained and complete seriousness for which among his pro-
ductions it is unique."

culus. The crude but forceless simplicity of Gradgrind can scarcely be said to represent the complexity and solidity of Bentham's influential contributions to English thought. Gradgrind is the merest of straw men. But it may well be that in writing *Hard Times* Dickens was impelled as much by a need to dissociate himself fully and publicly from the Benthamites as by any need to attack them for themselves.[8] The chief grounds on which he attacks the Benthamites, however, are well taken grounds — are, in fact, the very grounds on which Mill himself was to attack them two decades later in his *Autobiography*. Mill had to discover poetry in order to recover from the ravages of the Benthamite education imposed on him by his father; and the ultimate deficiency of the Gradgrind system, too, is that it ignores or condemns the imagination.

More interesting than the attack on the Benthamites, then, though it is laid out almost as obviously, is the defense of fancy and imagination. The necessity for imagination becomes clear only when the inadequacy of reason and of rational social action to deal completely with the unalterable aspects of existence is recognized. The death of fancy is linked to the threat of revolution:

The poor you will always have with you. Cultivate in them, while there is yet time, the utmost graces of the fancies and affections, to adorn their lives so much in need of ornament; or, in the days of your triumph, when romance is utterly driven out of their souls, and they and a bare existence stand face to face, Reality will take a wolfish turn, and make an end of you.

[8] See A. V. Dicey, *Law and Public Opinion in England* (London, 1905), pp. 418–22.

It is only imagination, too, that can bridge the gulf of difference between the classes, only imagination that can merge immediate and divergent self-interests in an ultimate common self-interest. "The like of you don't know us, don't care for us, don't belong to us," Rachael says to Louisa, and the "facts" of Coketown amply support her contention, though in Louisa's case the birth of her imaginative powers is accompanied by a growing realization of and sympathy for the condition of the poor.

Fancy is the progenitor of charity, in the Christian rather than the philanthropic sense, and it is the lack of fancy in her childhood that makes it impossible for Louisa to approach her mother's deathbed with full feeling, with better than "a heavy, hardened kind of sorrow." This recognition immediately precedes one of Dickens' most brilliant and functional death scenes, the death of Mrs. Gradgrind with only Louisa present.

"But there is something — not an Oology at all — that your father has missed, or forgotten, Louisa. I don't know what it is. I have often sat with Sissy near me, and thought about it. I shall never get its name now. But your father may. It makes me restless. I want to write to him, to find out for God's sake, what it is. Give me a pen, give me a pen."

Even the power of restlessness was gone, except from the poor head, which could just turn from side to side.

She fancied, however, that her request had been complied with, and that the pen she could not have held was in her hand. It matters little what figures of wonderful no-meaning she began to trace upon her wrappers. The hand soon stopped in the midst of them; the light that had always been feeble and dim behind the weak transparency, went out; and even Mrs. Gradgrind, emerged from the shadow in which man walketh

and disquieteth himself in vain, took upon her the dread
solemnity of the sages and patriarchs.

Here, as usual with Dickens, death is the control by
which reality is measured — and, in this case, by which
the Gradgrind system is discounted. In the vivid imaginative rendering of the scene, we comprehend what
forces are at work on Louisa to pierce her trained inca-
pacity, as we do too when her hazard at the devices of
James Harthouse is rendered in an extraordinary sexual
image: "The figure descended the great stairs, steadily,
steadily; always verging, like a weight in deep water, to
the black gulf at the bottom."

It is finally the brief, largely figurative renderings of
experience in this novel, far more than the rather mechanical working out of the plot, that most effectively
accomplish the destruction of the "hard facts" point of
view. We know best what is wrong with Coketown not
from the facts we are told about it, nor from the picture
of Bounderby's hypocritical oppression, nor even so
much from the scene of the union meeting, as from the
descriptive imagery of serpents and elephants. In a sense,
imagination makes its own best case for itself.

The great virtues of the novel are in disquieting part
incidental virtues — incidental, that is, to the main line
of development of the story, though absolutely essential
to its impact. The questions this raises are peculiar questions concerning the forced restriction of the play of
imagination or fancy in a novel that has chiefly to do with
the necessity for the free life of the imagination. It seems
almost Gradgrindian therefore to prefer *Hard Times* to,
say, *David Copperfield* or *Our Mutual Friend*!

A Tale of Two Cities

If the attack on the Benthamites is not the most valu-
able part of *Hard Times*, neither are we likely to value
A Tale of Two Cities most as a picture of the French
Revolution. Dickens wrote best from intimate knowledge, particularly in the matter of setting, and it is precisely the density and authority of such knowledge that
his French scene lacks, despite such moments as those of
the Carmagnole, or the sharpening of weapons in the
courtyard of Tellson's Bank, or the procession of the
tumbrils. It is only necessary to compare the trial scene
in *Great Expectations* with the two trial scenes in *A
Tale of Two Cities* to comprehend the issue precisely.
Though the scenes in *A Tale of Two Cities* have, in fact,
rather more dramatic potentiality, they are treated comparatively abstractly and summarily, and Dr. Manette's
testament is conceived and given as an interpolation
rather than as testimony read in court. Nor, despite the
insistence of the title and of the opening paragraphs, does
the situation of France before and during the Revolution seem to impinge very sharply on the situation of
England in the mid-nineteenth century.

In fact, the literal insistence is pretty much dropped
after the title and opening pages, and an analogy of a
more general sort emerges instead. In this analogy Darnay is an important link, not only because of his mixed
Anglo-French parentage (an attribute he shares with
Lucy Manette), but through his political and social interests, and symbolically at least by his name, Evre-
monde, which is a clear if unfounded and unlinguistic
play on Everyman. The intention, though not consist-

ently implemented, is occasionally very apparent, as in
the opening of the chapter entitled "Fifty-Two" (Book
VII, Chapter 13), when Darnay is awaiting execution:

In the black prison of the Conciergerie, the doomed of the
day awaited their fate. They were in number as the weeks
of the year. Fifty-two were to roll that afternoon on the
life tide of the city to the boundless everlasting sea. Before
their cells were quit of them, new occupants were appointed;
before their blood ran into the blood spilled yesterday, the
blood that was to mingle with theirs to-morrow was already
set apart.

Two score and twelve were told off. From the farmer-gen-
eral of seventy, whose riches could not buy his life, to the
seamstress of twenty, whose poverty and obscurity could not
save her. Physical diseases, engendered in the vices and ne-
glects of men, will seize on victims of all degrees; and the
frightful moral disorder, born of unspeakable suffering, in-
tolerable oppression, and heartless indifference, smote equally
without distinction.

Much combines here, in addition to Darnay's French
name, to implement the force of generalization: the
number fifty-two itself, "as the weeks of the year";
the fact that these fifty-two are only one day's increment
in a continuous river of blood; the actual invocation of
Dickens' obsessive image of life as a river running into the
"boundless everlasting sea"; and the use too of the *Bleak
House* image of the fruits of social injustice as a pesti-
lence that strikes rich and poor, lofty and obscure alike,
without regard to immediate guilt or innocence, a
"frightful moral disorder."

The greatest imaginative energy of *A Tale of Two
Cities* is suggested, by a title, once more, that Dickens

considered and rejected: "Buried Alive." His only great hope for the "frightful moral disorder" of the world lay, imaginatively if not doctrinally, in some kind of moral and vital regeneration, and the reiterated and varied playing on themes of regeneration and resurrection in *A Tale of Two Cities* provides the strongest line of imaginative coherence in this too often superficial novel. The elements that constitute the thematic line vary greatly in weight, ranging from comedy to ultimate gravity.

In the very first chapter, the message that Mr. Lorry has Jerry Cruncher convey back to Tellson's is "RE-CALLED TO LIFE." Dr. Manette is in fact recalled to life from a living death into which he can relapse under sufficient strain, and which for many years at least he can only stave off with an effort that he cannot even relinquish when he sleeps. Darnay too, in prison, thinks " 'Now am I left, as if I were dead.' Stopping then, to look down at the mattress, he turned from it with a sick feeling, and thought 'And here in these crawling creatures is the first condition of the body after death.' "

Sidney Carton tells Lucy Manette that he is "like one who died young. All my life might have been." His life having been a kind of death, it is appropriate that his death should be the beginning of his life and that he should die repeating Christ's promise to Martha of resurrection for the faithful. A comic rendering of the same theme is provided by Jerry Cruncher, who by night plies the trade of "Resurrection Man," and who is led by self-interest to the conviction that though it's "hard enough" of the law to execute a criminal, it's "wery hard" to quarter him and thereby "spile him." In this same comic exploitation of the theme of regeneration or resurrection, the spy Cly is the false Lazarus, who has risen from his grave easily enough because he has never been placed in it, and who has been saved from death by his simulated burial.

The theme of personal regeneration has the utmost pertinence for the general or historical meaning of a novel that testifies to the sufficient and miserable causes for revolution, but in which revolution itself accomplishes and is capable of accomplishing nothing but butchery, aggravating rather than relieving misery. Defarge comforts the father of the child killed by the Marquis's carriage by telling him that it is "better for the poor little plaything to die so, than to live. It has died in a moment without pain. Could it have lived an hour as happily?" This is the much reiterated statement of *Bleak House*, which concerns itself also with redemption. The brother of the girl whom the Marquis's brother has forced to become his mistress summons the Marquis and all his "bad race" to answer for their crimes in "the days when all these things are to be answered for"; and Doctor Manette ends his testament with the same summons.

The condition of the French people prior to the Revolution is pictured as a terrestrial hell — the condition ascribed to life more or less consistently in all the novels of Dickens' maturity, but with great literalness here. An extraordinary number of the French scenes, starting properly with the very first French scene, of the bloody wine spilled in the streets, are infernal. This hellishness is in substantial part man-made, the result of injustice and oppression. But Dickens is never sentimental about the victims of oppression. No transfer of power will change hell to heaven, for the plague of "the frightful moral disorder" has corrupted oppressors and oppressed equally, if not uniformly. The only genuine answer is both distant and radical, a profound regeneration of the human spirit. In this sense, the novel is a tale not so much of two cities as of all places, and it is possibly the great appeal of the theme of regeneration that makes this thin and often mawkish novel far more widely read than are most of the better novels Dickens wrote.

The Mystery of Edwin Drood

At least two large and intriguing questions are raised by the unfinished novel on which Dickens was at work at the time of his death: how did he mean to complete the story; and to what extent does it represent a break with a genre of fiction he had himself created, a break more than the ordinary for a writer so richly endowed with originality and invention that he never did the same thing twice. The evidence for anything like a definitive answer to either of these questions does not exist, which of course makes speculation about them both more enticing and less satisfactory; and though the first question has received more attention than the second, the second is far more interesting.

A general view of society in terms of which the story gains meaning is surely not entirely missing in *The Mystery of Edwin Drood*, but it figures as an informing force significantly less in this novel than in *Great Expectations* or *Our Mutual Friend*, the two preceding novels. The difference might have been reduced by the unwritten portion of the novel, but it could scarcely have been eliminated. As unclear as the extent of the difference is the degree of intention behind this differ-

ence, and, relatedly, the import of that intention. Did
Dickens himself, for example, consider *The Mystery of
Edwin Drood* an artistic advance or a necessary reduc-
tion of ambition? His extreme difficulties in sustaining
and completing *Our Mutual Friend* had shown him the
fatigue of his powers. The intervening four years had
not been a period of recovery for him. In his agreement
with the publisher Frederick Chapman for *The Mystery
of Edwin Drood*, there was included for the first time,
at Dickens' request, a clause dealing with the contin-
gency of his death before the completion of the manuscript. He intended, further, to write the story in only
twelve monthly parts, rather than the twenty monthly
parts that had been his favorite form of composition. If
The Mystery of Edwin Drood was a forced retreat —
a speculation that the evidence at least makes possible —
the matter is of biographical rather than critical interest,
and the novel might be excused from the kind of examination that the other novels deserve.

The Mystery of Edwin Drood can be considered an
advance, if at all, only as a less encumbered dealing with
the criminal mind than was possible in any of the denser
novels. There is greater insistence, too, on the unique-
ness of that mind. Dickens reinforces the point in a
parenthetical explanation. Rosa's incompetence to deal
with Jasper is in good part caused, he tells us, by her
ignorance of "the criminal intellect, which its own professed students perpetually misread, because they persist
in trying to reconcile it with the average intellect of
average men, instead of identifying it as a horrible
wonder apart." But in what does the greater isolation
of the picture consist, and what does it gain?

John Jasper and Bradley Headstone are unmistakably
similar conceptions, both of them men of talent and of
respectable though scarcely lofty situation. Both have
ambitions rather restricted by the positions they occupy (Jasper suggests to his nephew that this is the root
of his discontent), and both are rendered criminal by
frustrated sexual passion. But Headstone, unlike Jasper,
has risen from the lower classes, and he sees his failure
to win Lizzie, and Wrayburn's success in this same enterprise, as a question not of virtue or deserving, but of
class superiority and class privilege. Wrayburn wins the
girl because he is a gentleman, and Headstone is not.
That Lizzie herself is of the lower classes, of a lower
class even than Headstone, only aggravates the situation.

No such class difference enters into the opposition
between John Jasper and Edwin Drood, an opposition
that is unconscious on Drood's side, as it is ignored on
Wrayburn's. But again the successful man is the man
who might appear to deserve the girl less. Rosa comes to
Drood only as his willed portion, by a bequest that im-
pedes the very feelings it was intended to foster, which
might otherwise have developed quite naturally. The relationship between Rosa and Drood thus combines elements of both the Lizzie-Headstone-Wrayburn story
and the Harmon–Bella Wilfer story in *Our Mutual Friend*.
But the thematic matrices provided by the elaborately
calculated considerations of money, class, and marriage
in *Our Mutual Friend* give to personal relationships in
that novel a general social import that they do not possess
in *The Mystery of Edwin Drood*.

Surely pertinent to both Lizzie's rejection of Head-

stone and Rosa's disgusted fear of Jasper are those feelings of repugnance that that dissatisfied, deserving, and
violent man Charles Dickens seems to have inspired in
Ellen Ternan. But it is at best doubtful that the reduc-
tion of social import, of general social relevance, makes
more vivid the terror and pity of the personal situation.

There is, to be sure, new material in *The Mystery of
Edwin Drood* not found in the earlier novels, particularly
the Eastern material — opium, hypnosis, the occult facul-
ties of the Landless twins, the rituals and practices of the
Thugs. Yet all the ingenuity and intelligence that have
been expended on elaborating and explaining this material, interesting though much of it is in itself, serve more
than anything else to show that with so much of the
book unwritten, it is not really possible to grasp the genuine significance of these materials — to know, that is,
what Dickens would have made of them. The novel in
monthly parts, even in the reduced form employed in
this case, develops slowly; and here the elements have
been introduced and advanced, but they have not yet
been wizarded together, the novel is still to be made.

In addition to the new materials, there are many staples — the river and death by drowning; hypocritical
philanthropy and genuine benevolence; the cozy and
macabre jostling each other closely; vivid, mannered portraits of eccentricity. But if the elements seem something of a hotchpotch, the masterful certainty of the
story is nonetheless beyond doubt. From the opening
scene in the opium den to the last completed scene, in
which the old hag who operates the den discovers Jasper's identity, the interest scarcely lags, and the reader
is impelled forward on what he confidently believes to

be a straight path of discovery. Only he discovers comparatively little along the way, and since the end is never reached, the trip turns out to be a little disappointing. The rich undercurrent of suggestion, thematic and metaphorical, that sustains the greater novels of Dickens' maturity, is largely lacking here, where a tired but highly conscious and wily novelist seems to have fallen back primarily on his undiminished ability to tell a gripping story. The ambition is reduced, but the result is far less discouraging than a faltering attempt at the once possible would have been.

Deviation reinforces the outlines of the norm. So, among Dickens' novels, the sports help to define what is more generic. Such a distinction is possible only with a writer whose work bulks considerably. It is necessary too, or at least desirable, that the bulk itself of the accomplishment enter into our critical estimation. Each of Dickens' novels is autonomous and stands firmly in isolation. Yet any one of them is less without the reference provided by some knowledge of the others. There is unfortunately no exact word in English, as there is in French, to convey the concept of an artist's accomplishment as a whole, his artistic life. Even less do we have conceptual or evaluative terms for the difference between a total work of one or two important books, and a total work of a dozen or more. The English critical vocabulary reflects an embarrassment, as at grossness, at the idea of quantitative consideration of any sort.

So, too, we are largely unable to deal with physical magnitude in any single work, save for an understandable but nonetheless perverse prejudice in favor of the absence of magnitude, in favor of smallness. Concision is a virtue, but a very long novel can be made of concise parts; and though Dickens sometimes overwrites, his novels would still be very long if all the overwriting were eliminated. For accumulation is one of the mainstays of his method. In the densely populated world of his novels, statistics have importance. Twelve bad parents in a story signify something quite different from one bad parent — particularly if each of the twelve has a markedly different but related badness. The point and its reference to Dickens' fiction are too simple to labor.

In the shorter novels, with the exception of *Great Expectations*, the degree of accumulation is insufficient, which gives an arbitrary, sometimes inconsequential, but more often unjustifiably insistent air to much of the action. A single Gradgrind is an individual fool. A dozen Gradgrindian fools might suggest an intellectual epidemic, a social threat. Reiteration is one method of generalization, though scarcely the only one. Nor is it the only method of generalization, or extension of meaning, that Dickens himself employs. Clearly the principle of varied reiteration cannot be exploited to its logical conclusion. Art cannot create a one-for-one semblance of the world. Even any single semblance it creates is created by selection. To the extent that the principles of selection used in all instances in a work of art bear a relation to each other, the work has style and conveys a sufficient point of view. The consistency and pressure of Dickens' point of view — most plainly conveyed by his great social themes, but also by such repeated conjunctions as that of miserliness and impotence, or poverty and disease, or misery and violence — give all his fiction an unmistakable style. A further force of coherence is provided by his overseeing or encompassing themes: death as the central fact of life, for example; or the ambiguous line between reality and illusion; or the need for spiritual regeneration, and the terms in which such regeneration is possible. This combination of multitudinousness and control, extension and comprehension, supports a special version of literary realism.

Naturalistic, Dickens surely neither is nor attempts to be. Nor, similarly, is he bound to historical scrupulousness. He can ascribe to a single time, circumstances that belong in fact to substantially different times.[9] This may in part be carelessness, inattention, but it is at least as much to the point that these breaches of historical decorum are in the interest of the consistency and generalizing power of the created story. The defenders of poetry have traditionally contended that the freedom of poetry to tamper purposefully with literal truth, a license forbidden to history, is precisely what makes available to poetry a greater truth than is available to history. The modern historian circumvents this limitation considerably, and creates interpretive clarity by playing different times against one another for both analogy and contrast. Dickens manages a similar clarification by telescoping and superimposing. Appearance often obscures reality, and Dickens' novels came to more meaningful terms with the reality of his own day than did more literally realistic novels; and they continue to come to meaningful terms with the reality of our time when those other novels have long been museum pieces.

Topical allusions to different epochs are joined to

[9] As Humphry House has shown.

freer inventions and given coherence by the imagination that sees their connections and conveys those connections, thematically and symbolically, in the total
structure of the novel. It has been pointed out, for example, by Humphry House,[10] that in *Little Dorrit* Dickens sets the story in the 1820's, and uses for his Marshalsea scenes his memories of his father's imprisonment
there in that decade. But the Circumlocution Office is
based on the "administrative muddles of the Crimean
War" (1854–56), and Merdle is based on "John Sadleir,
the Tipperary banker [who] failed and committed suicide in 1856." This and other such combinations suggest
to House a "provisional rule . . . . that whatever may be
the imaginary date of the plot, the material most likely
to be contemporary with the time of writing, and most
topical to it, is the 'Reformism' and the more deliberate
social satire."

Though the logic of this is apparent, the distinction
suggested may be too sharp, for by the time of *Little
Dorrit* and earlier, Dickens had largely abandoned that
impulse for reform that had formerly led him in his novels to seek out specific and immediate abuses for correction. Though he wished surely in *Little Dorrit* to
show the evils of speculative enterprise and government
bureaucracy, his greatest effort was given to larger and
less immediate aims, having to do with the relation of
physical to psychological imprisonment, and with a kin-
dred exploration of the ambiguous distinction between
reality and illusion. For these reasons, his feelings about
his own experience of poverty and imprisonment in youth
(very close in many ways to the feelings of Amy Dorrit)

[10] Pp. 28–29.

are appropriately joined with his feelings about the im-
prisoning postures of money and bureaucracy, of which
his direct experience had been more recent. What is important — and perhaps realistic is not an inappropriate
word either — is the connection he sees between the
world of poverty of his youth and his experience of the
world of wealth and position in maturity. Like most
writers of fiction, he uses the smaller, more intense world
of youthful memory as a control from which to move
out to the larger, more diffuse world of maturity. The
size of his novels is further justified by their spaciousness.

The lesson Dickens took from his own life — as
ascertainable in *Little Dorrit* as anywhere — was that the
grim view imposed on him in childhood by immediate
circumstances was in fact an accurate, a realistic view,
save that the causes were more profound than he then
knew, harder to correct even than poverty and neglect.
For a time in his early manhood, success and his great
energy deflect him from what he still knows nonetheless,
even if unadmittedly. But by his middle years, he has
brought together the two experiences, of deprived youth
and successful manhood, into a single coherent and hellish
vision. His repeated effort, in his mature fiction, is to find
a means to convey this vision in its "truth" (to use the
word he used in this sense himself), and as nearly as
possible in its entirety.

Dickens' early novels are products of his period of
relative optimism, when he could dissociate himself
somewhat from the sufferings of his childhood because
he did not yet understand that they were only an introduction to the sufferings of adulthood. In these years,
in the exploitation of his social themes, he writes about

deprivation as something of which people can and should be relieved, in order to enjoy the well-being he now enjoys himself. When this honeymoon with success is over — and the period is not really a very long one, even though the output in this time is enormous — he still attacks social injustice indefatigably, but he sees man's basic suffering as beyond the power of money or legislation to relieve, as a pervasive and blighting spiritual disorder.

The dark view that even at his most optimistic moments is just beneath the surface, surfaces, and informs everything he writes with increasingly conscious purpose and by increasingly conscious means. In this period, extension even by great accumulation of detail cannot create the totality he intends, and he turns, not instead but in addition, to the employment of highly stylized means — among others, of naturalistic symbols. By these combined means he creates in his mature novels a totality, aspiring to the diversity and magnitude of the actual world and paying testimony to its mystery, but finding meaning and coherence in its apparent confusion.

INDEX

Accident, Dickens on, 19–20

Accumulation, characteristic of Dickens' method, 184–186, 189

All the Year Round, 3, 8n, 11, 15, 27, 34, 49, 51, 54, 58, 61, 62, 63; comments on stories submitted to, 18, 20, 21; attacks literary conventions, 22–23, 25; on industry, 69

Alton Locke, 23

American Notes, 95

Anticipation, Dickens on, 19–20

Aristocracy: Dickens on, 46, 47; in *Little Dorrit*, 129; in *Our Mutual Friend*, 137

Art: and popularity, 6; and reality, 9–11, 22–23, 185–186; Dickens' view, 19; and originality, 23–25; social purpose, 26–32, 189; novel as, 36; and social novels, 107

Artful Dodger, 89, 93

Authority: in *Bleak House*, 124; in *David Copperfield*, 153–155

Autobiography: in *Bleak House*, 124–125; in *David Copperfield*, 146, 153; in *Great Expectations*, 146

Badger, Mr. Bayham, 123

Bagehot, Walter, 63

"Bagman's Story, The," 83

Bagnet, Mrs., 125

Balzac, Honoré de, 8

Banks, joint-stock, 61–62, 63, 64–66

Bardell, Mrs., 80, 81, 82

Bardell, vs. Pickwick, 76, 79, 80–81

Barkis, 147, 150, 156

Barnaby Rudge, 95, 101–103

Baudelaire, Charles, 24

Beggar's Opera, compared to *Oliver Twist*, 94

Benevolence: as theme, 97, 183; in *Nicholas Nickleby*, 98; and money, 98, 101, 104; in *Old Curiosity Shop*, 100–101; in *Barnaby Rudge*, 103; in *Martin Chuzzlewit*, 104; in *Dombey and Son*, 116; in *Our Mutual Friend*, 137

Bentham, Jeremy, 42, 51n, 52, 173

Benthamites: and Poor Law of 1834, 52, 54, 55; attacked in *Hard Times*, 171, 172–173, 176

Bentley's Magazine, 86

Biddy, 147, 162, 163, 167

Blandois, 130

Blatton, Mr., 88

Bleak House, 15, 107, 132, 155, 179; preface to, 10; social symbols in, 106; death theme in, 109, 117–119; possible titles for, 119; epidemic in, 120, 121, 126; social injustice in, 120–123, 177; ignorance in, 123–124; responsibility in, 124–126

Blimbers, the, 114

Bob (*Little Dorrit*), 128

Boffins, the, 135, 136, 137, 141

Bottle, The (Cruikshank), 30

Bounderby, Josiah, 175

Shop, 100; in *Barnaby Rudge*, 102–103; in *Martin Chuzzlewit*, 104; in *Little Dorrit*, 130, 187–188; in *Our Mutual Friend*, 137
Gowan, Henry, 130
Gradgrind, Louisa, 174–175
Gradgrind, Mr., 133, 173, 175, 185
Gradgrind, Mrs., 174
Grant, Daniel and William, 98
Great Expectations, 12, 87, 106, 170, 180; ending, 7, 166–168; parallels with *David Copperfield*, 146–148, 163, 168; compared to *Paradise Lost*, 156–158, 168; innocence in, 158–159; property in, 159–161; love in, 162–163; fate and justice in, 163–166; length of, 171
Gride, Arthur, 97, 98
Gridley, Mr., 124
Guppy, 118

Hall, William, 75
Hamlet, 24
Hard Times, 15, 52, 85, 87, 100, 106, 133; Dickens on, 29; short form of, 170–171; Benthamites in, 171, 172–173; modern taste for, 172; fancy and imagination in, 173–175
Harmon, John, 134, 135, 136, 137, 142, 182
Harmon, Old, 135, 136, 140
Harthouse, James, 175
Havisham, Miss, 147, 159, 160–161, 162, 166
Hawdon, Captain, 126
Hawk, Sir Mulberry, 99
Headstone, Bradley, 136, 144; compared to John Jasper, 170, 182
Heep, Uriah, 155, 156
Henry IV, 17
Hexam, Charley, 135, 136, 139, 140

Hexam, Gaffer, 136, 139, 140, 141, 142, 143
Hexam, Lizzie, 134, 135, 136, 137, 139, 140, 141–142, 143, 182
Hide and Seek, 25
Higden, Betty, 135, 137, 143
History, Dickens' view, 69, 186–187
House, Humphry, 67, 187
House of Commons, 92, 137, 155; Dickens' view of, 37, 40
Household Narrative, The, 10, 23, 34, 36, 70, 71
Household Words, 3, 11, 15, 27, 29, 31, 34, 54, 56, 58; on beauty and ugliness, 9; attacks snobbery, 12–13, 44; comments on stories submitted to, 18, 23, 25, 26; attacks conventions, 22, 24; attacks government, 37, 38, 39; on strikes, 47, 48, 49; on poverty, 51; attacks money, 59, 61, 62; on industry, 69, 70; dust symbol in, 134
Hugh the ostler, 102
Humours, 17
Humphry Clinker, 5
Hypocrisy: and money, 60–61; in *David Copperfield*, 156; in *Great Expectations*, 168; in *Edwin Drood*, 183

Ignorance, in *Bleak House*, 120, 123–124
Illustrators, 15–16
Imagination: and facts, 14–15, 187; in *David Copperfield* and *Great Expectations*, 168; in *Hard Times*, 173–175
Imprisonment, in *Little Dorrit*, 109, 126, 187–188. *See also* Prison scenes
Independence, 57
Industrial accidents, 70
Industry, 36; Dickens' attitude, 59, 60, 67; and need for capital, 61–

relation of plot to character, 18–21; originality, 22–25; entertainment, 26; social purpose, 26–32, 187–189

Littimer, 155

Little Dorrit, 10, 82, 108, 134, 171n; social symbols in, 106–107; imprisonment theme, 109, 126, 187–188; reality versus illusion in, 127–132

Little Nell, 11, 100, 101

Liz, 117

Lloyds, 63

London: slum described, 13–14; sense of in novels, 15, 77–78

Lorry, Mr., 178

Love: theme in *Dombey and Son*, 112; in *Great Expectations*, 162–163, 168

Lower class. *See* Laboring class

Lytton, Bulwer, 7, 21, 42, 167

Macbeth, 25

Machines. *See* Industry

Macready, William C., 39

"Madman's Manuscript, A," 82–83

Magazines: social views in, 34–35; serialization problems, 86–89. *See also* by name

Magwitch, 147, 159, 161, 162, 163; trial of, 164–166

Maldon, Jack, 150

Manette, Dr., 176, 178, 179

Manette, Lucy, 176, 178

Mann, Mrs., 93

Mantalinis, the, 98

Marigold, Dr., 11

Marriages: unseemly, as theme in *Nicholas Nickleby*, 97, 98–99; in *Old Curiosity Shop*, 101; in *Barnaby Rudge*, 103; in *Martin Chuzzlewit*, 104–105; in *Dombey and Son*, 116; in *Our Mutual Friend*, 134–135, 137; in *Edwin Drood* and *Our Mutual Friend* compared, 182

Marshalsea, 106, 127–128, 129, 131, 187

Martha, 150, 156

Martin Chuzzlewit, 103–105, 109

Martineau, Harriet, 25, 26, 28

Marx, Karl, 43

Master Humphrey's Clock, 95

Maylie, Harry, 92

McHenry, James, 67

Mell, Mr., 149, 155

Memorandum Book, Dickens', 132

Merdle, Mr., 128, 130, 134, 187

Merry Wives of Windsor, The, 17, 18

Meyerbeer, Giacomo, 26

Micawber, Mr., 149

Micawber family, 147, 156

Middle class: Dickens' views on, 7–8, 39, 46; in *Sketches by Boz*, 78

Mill, John Stuart, 173

Milton, John, 157

Miserliness, 185

Misery, 78, 81, 185; in *Oliver Twist*, 89–90; in *Bleak House*, 121, 124; in *Little Dorrit*, 128–129, 132; in *Our Mutual Friend*, 138. *See also* Injustice; Poverty

Molly, 164, 166

Money, 36; Dickens' attitude toward, 59–67, 96; in *Nicholas Nickleby*, 96, 97–98; in *Old Curiosity Shop*, 96, 100; in *Martin Chuzzlewit*, 96, 103–104; and benevolence, 98, 101, 104; in *Dombey and Son*, 110–111, 116; in *Bleak House*, 120; in *Little Dorrit*, 128–129, 188; in *Our Mutual Friend*, 132, 134, 135, 137, 139–140, 141, 182; in *Edwin Drood*, 182

Moneylenders, 61

Monks, 91

Montague, 105

Moonstone, The, 25

Morality: and money, 60, 61; in

Wemmick, 147, 161, 163, 166
Wickfield, Agnes, 147, 150
Wilfer, Bella, 134, 135, 136, 142, 182
Wilfer, Mr., 136
Wilfer, Mrs., 136
Wills, W. H., 7, 14, 19, 20, 25, 35
Wilson, Edmund, 47, 91–92
Winkle, Mr., 77, 79, 80, 85
Woman in White, The, 6, 20

Woodcourt, Allan, 118, 121, 125
Workhouses, 92; and Poor Law of 1834, 54–55
Workingmen. *See* Laboring class
Wrayburn, Eugene, 134, 135, 136, 137, 140, 143–144, 182
Wren, Jenny, 135, 137, 138

Xenos, Stefanos, 65

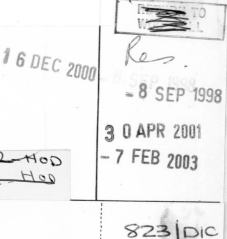

1670782

Engel

The Maturity
of Dickens

823/DIC

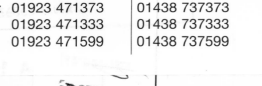

-2 SEP 1978

16 DEC 2000

-8 SEP 1998

30 APR 2001

-7 FEB 2003

2 FE

17 DEC ... 2 HOD

-2 SEP 1978 2 HOD

823/DIC